# Pieces and Pat...
# A Patchwork in Math and Sc...

by
Judith A. Hillen
Fresno Pacific College
Fresno, California

## ILLUSTRATIONS

by

Sheryl Mercier

## EDITORS

Arthur Wiebe
Project Director
Fresno Pacific College

Larry Ecklund
Project Director
Fresno Pacific College

Judith A. Hillen
Assoc. Project Director
Fresno Pacific College

AIMS (Activities Integrating Mathematics and Science) began in 1981 with a grant from the National Science Foundation. The non-profit AIMS Education Foundation publishes hands-on instructional materials (books and the monthly AIMS Newsletter) that integrate curricular disciplines such as mathematics, science, language arts, and social studies. The Foundation sponsors a national program of professional development through which educators may gain both an understanding of the AIMS philosophy and expertise in teaching by integrated, hands-on methods.

ISBN 1-881431-03-7

Printed in the United States of America

# Table of Contents

# Index of Skills

## MATH SKILLS

## SCIENCE PROCESSES

# I HEAR, AND I FORGET
# I SEE, AND I REMEMBER
# I DO, AND I UNDERSTAND

-Chinese Proverb

# Introduction

*A Patchwork in Math and Science* is an invitation for teachers and students to experience the joy of science through hands-on activities rooted in real world experiences. If we want children to understand science, we need to provide many opportunities for them to observe and compare, collect and organize, guess and test, build and analyze, and the freedom to say "I wonder what would happen if?" If they never wonder how and why, they will never know science.

When the learner becomes so engrossed in "doing as the scientist does", the rewards are many. The student becomes highly motivated to continue further pursuit of an experiment on his own. He also sees practical, real world applications of math skills. The "doing" process also encourages those students with poor reading ability to actively participate in this non-reading activity and feel very successful. Field testing results confirm the idea that when students work cooperatively in discovery oriented activities such as these, teachers are freed from having to know all the "right" answers. Instead, he or she becomes a facilitator skillful in guiding learners in a search for solutions. Students are now doing the sequencing, verbalizing and synthesizing.

The activities described on the following pages begin with the simplest of science processes, observing and classifying, and progress to the more complex approaches of applying and generalizing. A variety of topics from sunlight and shadows to mirrors and symmetry allows the teacher a certain amount of freedom with regard to sequence and selection of activities. A major consideration is that the activities presented here are mutually stimulating for both the learner and the teacher and that we are contributing to a broad base of remembered experiences where participants "do" and understand, not just see and hear the answers. Be encouraged that if each of us does his share of inviting children to know science, collectively we are enhancing and enriching their lives.

I. **Topic Area**

Classifying and sorting jelly beans.

II. **Introductory Statement**

Students will design and construct a circle graph to show color distribution of jelly beans.

III. **Math Skills**

a. Fractions
b. Circle graphs
c. Geometry
d. Using a protractor

**Science Processes**

a. Observing
b. Classifying
c. Recording data
d. Interpreting data

IV. **Materials**

Jelly Bellys (gourmet jelly beans)—36 jelly beans per group of five (5) students
Protractors
Colored pencils
Plastic sandwich baggies

V. **Key Question**

How can we create a circle graph that will show the color distribution in a set of jelly beans?

VI. **Educative Input**

Assorted Jelly Belly candies may be purchased in 8 oz. packages (approx. 200) for about $2.00. These candies are smaller than the regular jelly bean and come in an assortment of 15 colors and flavors.

VII. **Management Suggestions**

1. Randomly select 36 jelly beans and place in a plastic baggie.
2. One 8 oz. package of Jelly Bellys will be enough for about 5 sets of 36.
3. Students may work in pairs or in small groups.

VIII. **Procedure**

1. Distribute package of 36 Jelly Bellys to each small group.
2. Make a tally and record the number of each color in your sample.

3. Express as a fraction. The numerator will be the number of a specific color. The denominator will be the total number in the sample (36).
4. Convert each fraction, n/36, to an equivalent fraction with a denominator of 360. (Multiply by 10). We will call this new fraction a circle fraction.
5. Use a protractor to measure and construct each circle fraction within the circle graph.
6. Color each part to match the flavor and label all parts of the circle graph.

IX. **What the Students Will Do**

1. Observe and classify jelly beans according to color.
2. Record data in a table.
3. Construct a circle graph as a way of organizing data.
4. Interpret and generalize information from the circle graph.

X. **Discussion**

1. Compare the likenesses and differences of each sample.
2. How many colors (flavors) are represented in each sample? In all samples?
3. Does any one color appear more frequently than all the others?
4. Does any color represent exactly ½ of your sample? ¼? ⅓?

XI. **Extension**

1. Repeat this activity with any number of jelly beans that is a factor of 360 (i.e. 18, 54, 72, etc.) and construct a circle graph that represents the color distribution. Using a different number of jelly beans in the sample provides practice converting to equivalent fractions with a denominator of 360.
2. Convert each fraction to a percent. Make a circle graph and label with percentages.
3. Combine all samples and do a class graph. You may with to choose a different type of graph—bar or pictorial.

# Jelly Belly

Please sort jelly beans. Record data.

_____
Name

| COLOR | TALLY | TOTAL | RAW FRACTION $\frac{n}{total}$ | CIRCLE FRACTION $\frac{n \times 10}{360}$ |
|---|---|---|---|---|
| | | | | |
| | | | | |
| | | | | |
| | | | | |
| | | | | |
| | | | | |
| | | | | |
| | | | | |
| | | | | |
| | | | | |
| | | | | |
| | | | | |
| | | | | |
| Total | | | | |

2

PIECES AND PATTERNS

Name _____

# Constructing a Circle Graph

**1.** Let the circle represent the total number of jelly beans in your sample.

**2.** Use a protractor to measure a circle fraction to represent the number of each color in your sample.

**3.** Lightly color and label each part of your graph.

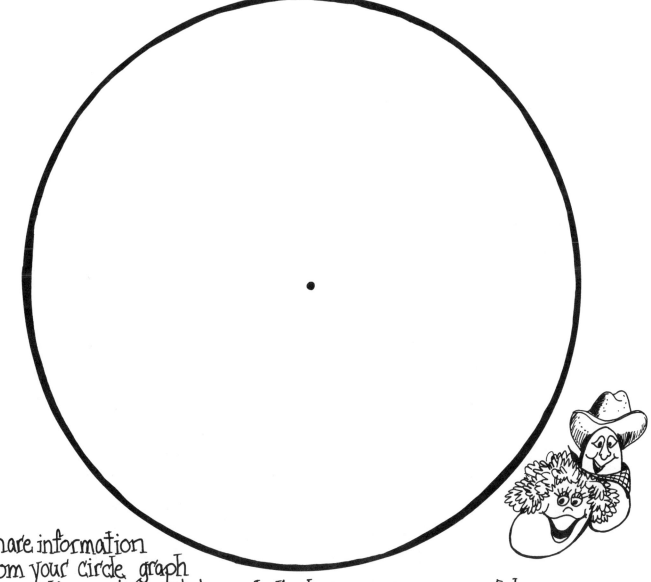

**4.** Share information from your circle graph by writing a true statement that summarizes your data.

_____
Name

# Constructing a Circle Graph

1. Let the circle represent the total number of jelly beans in your sample.

2. Use a protractor to measure a circle fraction to represent the number of each color in your sample.

3. Lightly color and label each part of your graph.

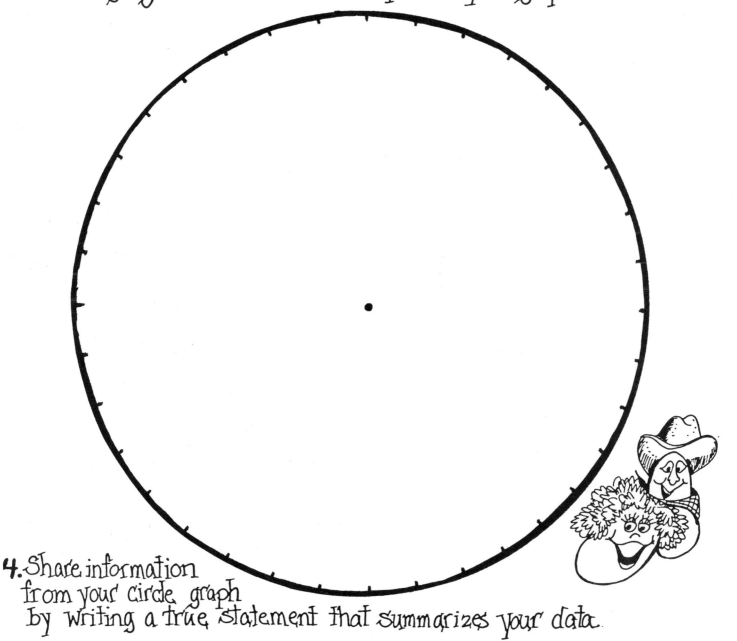

4. Share information from your circle graph by writing a true statement that summarizes your data.

_____

_____

# Button, Button

## I. Topic Area
Venn diagrams and attributes of buttons

## II. Introductory Statement
Students will use the attributes of an assortment of buttons to enhance the meaning of organizing and interpreting data using the Venn diagram.

## III. Math Skills
a. Attributes
b. Set theory
c. Problem solving
d. Logic

## Science Processes
a. Observing
b. Classifying
c. Organizing data
d. Interpreting data
e. Applying and generalizing

## IV. Materials
Assortment of buttons
Colored pencils or crayons
Scissors
Glue

## V. Key Question
Can you make a figure eight of buttons in which all adjacent buttons differ in only one way?

## VI. Educative Input
1. Using Venn diagrams is an appropriate and divergent way for students to organize and interpret information.
2. There are 3 main kinds of operations with sets presented in this series of worksheets: one set, two sets, and 2 or 3 intersecting sets.
3. Encourage students to describe attributes positively (all buttons in this set are red, round) and negatively using the not statement (these buttons are not red and not round).

## VII. Management Suggestions
1. Students may work effectively in groups of 3-5.
2. Each activity has two pages: the first page is very structured while the second page is open ended for creative follow-up. Activities include: one set, two sets, and intersecting sets followed by a Baffler.

## VIII. Procedure
1. Distribute buttons in packets of 10-20 per team.
2. Sort buttons according to the attributes listed on the worksheet: color, size, shape, and number of holes.
3. Record information in appropriate columns: Attribute and Number.
4. Cut out labels and "un-labels" for use on succeeding worksheets. Record appropriate information on empty labels.
5. Use labels and buttons to complete each activity as described on worksheets: one set, two sets, or intersecting sets.
6. Using the buttons, choose 1, 2, or 3 differences and try to conquer the Button Baffler by placing a button in each space so that each is different from its neighbor by one, two or three attributes.

## IX. What the Students Will Do
1. Sort buttons according to attributes.
2. Organize and record data in a Venn diagram format.
3. Interpret data and apply to a problem solving situation in open ended worksheets and the Button Baffler.

## X. Discussion
1. Discussion questions in these activities are included as an integral part of the worksheets.

## XI. Extensions
1. Make a list of other things to sort and classify. Choose one to do independently (leaves, shells, keys, bottle caps, pieces of fabric, etc.)
2. Apply your ability to sort and classify by completing this format with objects, pictures of objects, numbers, or symbols.

These are alike: ____ ____ ____
These are not alike: ____ ____ ____
Which of these are alike? ____ ____ ____

# Button, Button

Sort and classify your set of buttons according to color, size, shape, and number of holes.

## Labels for Venn Diagrams

| Attribute | Number | Label | Un-label |
|---|---|---|---|
| Color | | | |
| | | | not |
| | | | not |
| | | | not |
| | | | not |
| | | | not |
| total | | | |

| Size | Number | Label | Un-label |
|---|---|---|---|
| large (over 1cm diameter) | | large | not large |
| small | | small | not small |
| total | | | |

| Shape | Number | Label | Un-label |
|---|---|---|---|
| round | | round | not round |
| other | | | not |
| total | | | |

| Number of Holes | Number | Label | Un-label |
|---|---|---|---|
| one | | one | not one |
| two | | two | not two |
| four | | four | not four |
| total | | | |

6

# Button, Button

(One Set)

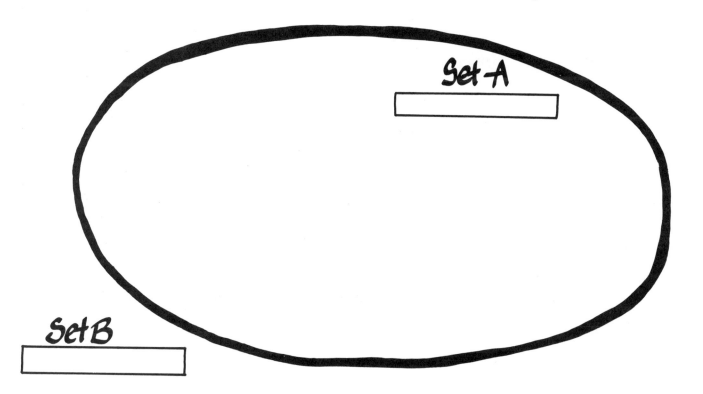

Set A

Set B

1. Sort all buttons by color (one attribute).
2. Place all buttons that are white inside the loop.
3. Place all other buttons (not white) outside the loop.
4. Trace and color all buttons in their proper places.
5. Label the set <u>inside</u> the loop and outside the loop.
6. How many buttons are white? _____
7. How many buttons are not white? _____
8. What is the total number of buttons? _____
9. Describe the set of buttons inside the loop by color and number: _____
10. Describe the set of buttons outside the loop by color and number: _____

PIECES AND PATTERNS

# Button, Button

(One Set 2.)

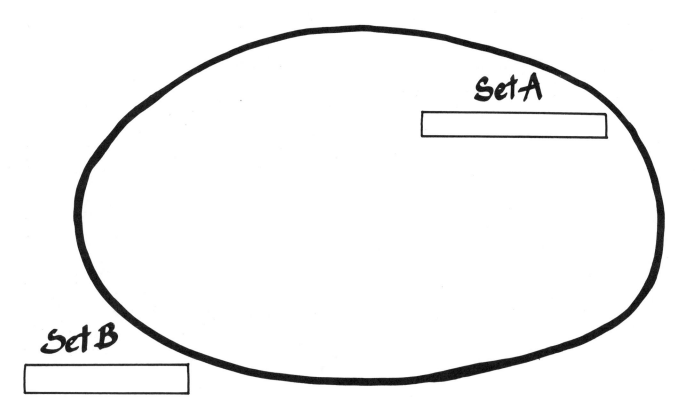

Set A

Set B

1. Sort the buttons according to one attribute.
2. Trace and color all buttons in the diagram.
3. Label all parts of the Venn Diagram.
4. Describe by attribute and number, the set inside the loop and outside the loop.

Set A : _____

Set B: _____

PIECES AND PATTERNS

# Button, Button

(Two Sets 1.)

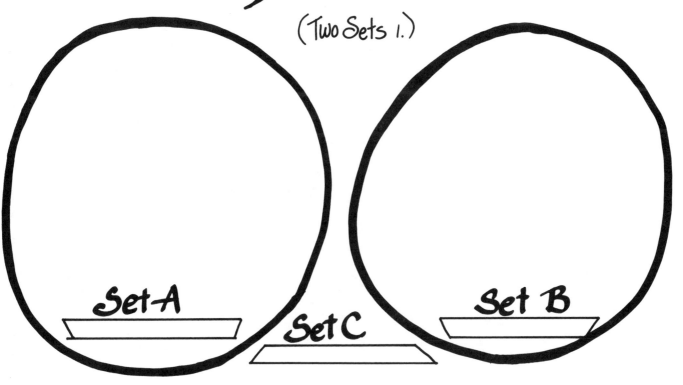

Set A     Set C     Set B

1. Sort all buttons according to number of holes (attribute = # of holes).
2. Place all buttons with 2 holes in Set A. Label the set.
3. Place all buttons with 4 holes in Set B. Label the set.
4. Place all buttons that do not have 2 holes or 4 holes outside Set A and Set B. Label the set.
5. Trace and color all the buttons in their place.
6. Complete the table:

| 2 holes | 4 holes | not 2 or 4 holes | Total |
|---------|---------|------------------|-------|
|         |         |                  |       |

7. Describe the set of buttons inside Set A by attribute (# of holes) and number: _____
8. Describe the set of buttons inside Set B by attribute (# of holes) and number. _____
9. Describe the set of buttons outside A+B (set C) by attribute (# of holes) and number. _____
_____

9

PIECES AND PATTERNS

# Button, Button

(Two Sets 2.)

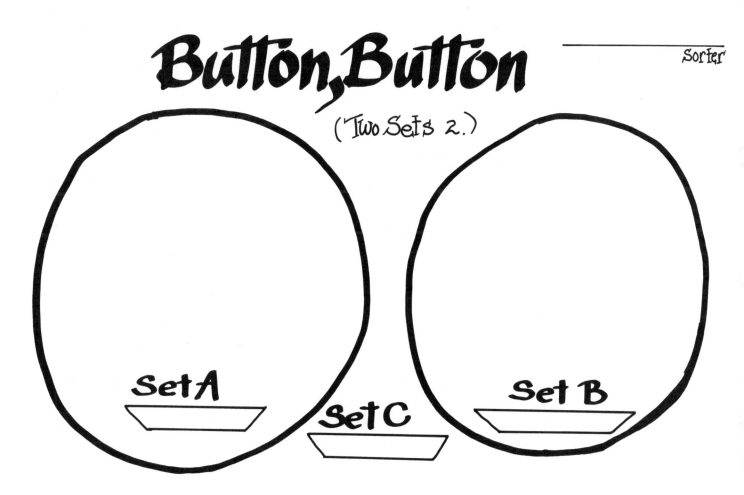

Set A

Set C

Set B

1. Sort all buttons according to one attribute.
2. Place and color all buttons in the diagram.
3. Label all sets.
4. Describe each set by attribute and number.

Set A: _____

Set B: _____

Set outside A & B: _____

10

© 1986 AIMS Education Foundation

**PIECES AND PATTERNS**

# Button,Button

Sorter

(Intersecting Sets)

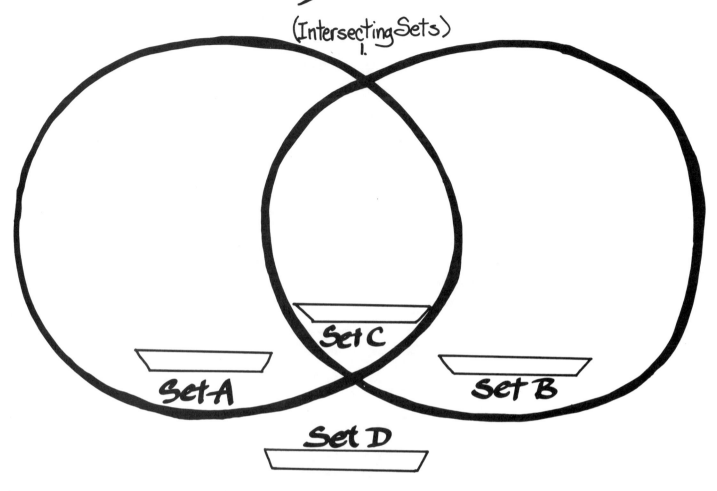

1. Sort buttons according to 2 attributes: size and color.
2. Place all large buttons in Set A ..... and label.
3. Place all blue buttons in Set B ... and label.
4. Place all buttons that are both large and blue in Set C and label.
5. Place all buttons that are not large and not blue outside the sets.
6. Trace and color all buttons.

Describe Set A by attribute and number:_____
Describe Set B by attribute and number:_____
Describe Set C by attribute and number:_____
Describe Set D by attribute and number:_____

© **1986 AIMS Education Foundation**

11

**PIECES AND PATTERNS**

# Button, Button

( Intersecting Sets )
2.

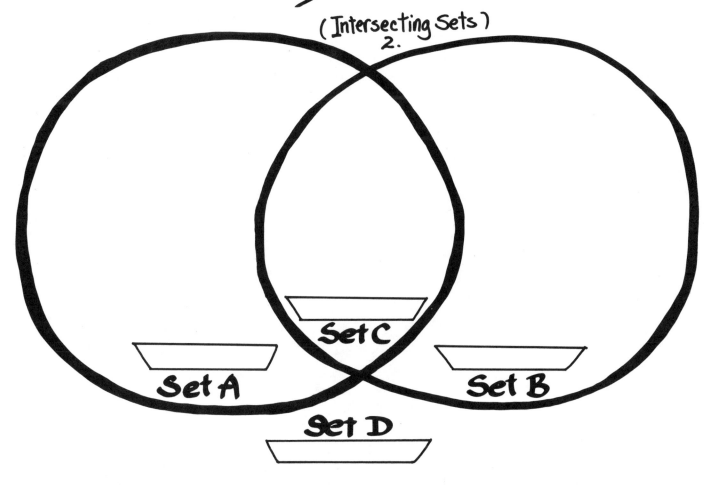

Set C

Set A

Set B

Set D

1. Sort buttons according to two attributes
   _____ and _____ .

2. Label each set.
3. Trace and color all buttons.
4. Describe each set by attribute and number:

Set A:_____

Set B:_____

Set C:_____

Set D:_____

12                **PIECES AND PATTERNS**

# Button, Button

(Intersecting Sets)

Set A

Set B

Set D

Set G

Set F

Set E

Set H

Set C

This is a real challenge! Sort and place buttons according to 3 attributes.
Trace and color all buttons.
Label the sets.
Describe each set according to attribute and number:

Set A: _____  Set E: _____

Set B: _____  Set F: _____

Set C: _____  Set G: _____

Set D: _____  Set H: _____

PIECES AND PATTERNS

# Button Baffler

Choose one

one difference
two differences
three differences

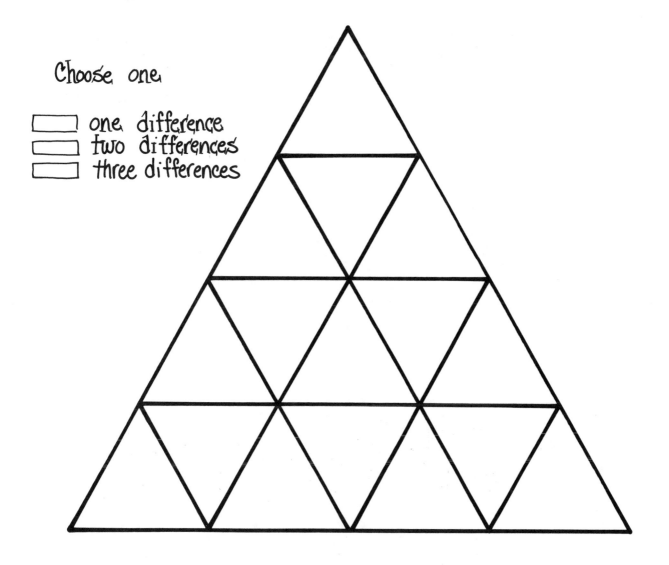

Place a button in each space so that each button is different from its neighbors by one, two, or three attributes.

# Trying Triangles

## I. Topic Area
Number cubes (dice) and probability.

## II. Introductory Statement
Students will roll three (3) cubes and determine whether the resulting numbers (which represent lengths of line segments) make it possible to construct a triangle. Students will also discover a pattern in predicting whether or not a group of numbers will construct a triangle.

## III. Math Skills
a. Properties of triangles
b. Classification of triangles
c. Addition
d. Problem solving
e. Predicting
f. Equalities and inequalities

## Science Processes
a. Classifying
b. Measuring
c. Predicting
d. Recording data
e. Interpreting data
f. Generalizing information

## IV. Materials
3 numbered cubes per group of 2-5 students (1-6 on each cube)
Plastic straws cut in these lengths: (Set of 18 straws per group)
    3-1 inch   3-3 inch   3-5 inch
    3-2 inch   3-4 inch   3-6 inch
Yarn or string for "threading" straws

## V. Key Question
Will any three (3) numbers rolled make a triangle?

## VI. Educative Input
1. Notice that the sum of the two (2) shorter sides must be greater than the longest side in order to construct a triangle.
2. There are 216 arrangements that may occur when rolling three dice. Of those there are many that are simple rearrangements of the same digits. For the sake of simplicity, we will use the 56 unique combinations for classifying whether or not a triangle can be formed.

## VII. Management Suggestions
1. Students should work in small groups of 2-5.
2. Demonstrate how straws must meet to form a triangle. Threading the straws and tying them together will form a triangle that can be hung as an example.

## VIII. Procedure
1. Each group will have a set of 18 straws and three dice.
2. Toss three dice. Determine if a triangle can be formed by matching the measured straws and trying to form a triangle by threading the straws together.
3. Record the numbers and results on the student worksheet.
4. Make a systematic record of all the possible outcomes that will result in a triangle.
5. Write a number sentence (equation) that generalizes the relationship for the numbers generated that form a triangle.

## IX. What the Students Will Do
1. Toss dice and attempt to construct a triangle from the resulting numbers.
2. Record data.
3. Interpret results.
4. Generalize concept of predicting whether or not three numbers will result in a triangle.

## X. Discussion
1. Which combinations of numbers will not result in the construction of a triangle? Why not?
2. What pattern of numbers results in the formation of a triangle? You may wish to initiate a guided discussion regarding this pattern. You might say, "I know a short cut that determines whether or not three numbers or lengths will form a triangle. Can you figure it out?" Imagine these lengths 1-1-6. Can you form a triangle? (No) Why? (The sum of the two shorter sides is not greater than the longest.) Imagine 1-2-6. Repeat. As you do this, record on the chalkboard in this manner:

| Side a | | Side b | | Side c | $\Delta$ |
|---|---|---|---|---|---|
| 1 | + | 1 | < | 6 | no |
| 1 | + | 2 | < | 6 | no |
| 1 | + | 3 | < | 6 | no |
| 1 | + | 4 | < | 6 | no |
| 1 | + | 5 | = | 6 | no |
| 1 | + | 6 | > | 6 | yes |

Let's let a and b represent the short sides and c the longest side of any triangle. At what point do we have a combination of numbers that results in a triangle? Can you use letters and a math symbol to express what you have discovered? $(a+b)>c$ equals a triangle.
3. How many triangles can be formed from the numbers rolled? See worksheet and mark each set of numbers that forms a triangle (34 of the 56 will result in a triangle.)
4. How can you organize and record all the possible outcomes that result in a triangle?

## XI. Extensions
1. See *See How They Roll* and *Probably Pythagorean.*

**PIECES AND PATTERNS**

# Trying Triangles

_____
Name

1. Roll 3 dice and match the numbers with straws of the same length.

2. Use the straws to construct triangles. Record.

3. Let <u>a</u> and <u>b</u> represent the shorter sides and <u>c</u> the longest side.

| Length of side <u>a</u> | Length of side <u>b</u> | Length of side <u>c</u> | Triangle △ yes or no |
|---|---|---|---|
|  |  |  |  |
|  |  |  |  |
|  |  |  |  |
|  |  |  |  |
|  |  |  |  |
|  |  |  |  |
|  |  |  |  |
|  |  |  |  |

4. Find 3 combinations of lengths that <u>will</u> <u>not</u> form a triangle:

___ ___ ___ , ___ ___ ___ , and ___ ___ ___ .

Find 3 combinations of lengths that <u>will</u> form a triangle:

___ ___ ___ , ___ ___ ___ , and ___ ___ ___ .

PIECES AND PATTERNS

# Trying Triangles

Name _____

Given these 56 possible outcomes when rolling 3 dice, label those that form a triangle.

| | | | | | | | | | | |
|---|---|---|---|---|---|---|---|---|---|---|
| 1 | 1 | 1 | | | 1 | 5 | 6 | | 3 | 3 | 5 | |
| 1 | 1 | 2 | | | 1 | 6 | 6 | | 3 | 3 | 6 | |
| 1 | 1 | 3 | | | 2 | 2 | 2 | | 3 | 4 | 4 | |
| 1 | 1 | 4 | | | 2 | 2 | 3 | | 3 | 4 | 5 | |
| 1 | 1 | 5 | | | 2 | 2 | 4 | | 3 | 4 | 6 | |
| 1 | 1 | 6 | | | 2 | 2 | 5 | | 3 | 5 | 5 | |
| 1 | 2 | 2 | | | 2 | 2 | 6 | | 3 | 5 | 6 | |
| 1 | 2 | 3 | | | 2 | 3 | 3 | | 3 | 6 | 6 | |
| 1 | 2 | 4 | | | 2 | 3 | 4 | | 4 | 4 | 4 | |
| 1 | 2 | 5 | | | 2 | 3 | 5 | | 4 | 4 | 5 | |
| 1 | 2 | 6 | | | 2 | 3 | 6 | | 4 | 4 | 6 | |
| 1 | 3 | 3 | | | 2 | 4 | 4 | | 4 | 5 | 5 | |
| 1 | 3 | 4 | | | 2 | 4 | 5 | | 4 | 5 | 6 | |
| 1 | 3 | 5 | | | 2 | 4 | 6 | | 4 | 6 | 6 | |
| 1 | 3 | 6 | | | 2 | 5 | 5 | | 5 | 5 | 5 | |
| 1 | 4 | 4 | | | 2 | 5 | 6 | | 5 | 5 | 6 | |
| 1 | 4 | 5 | | | 2 | 6 | 6 | | 5 | 6 | 6 | |
| 1 | 4 | 6 | | | 3 | 3 | 3 | | 6 | 6 | 6 | |
| 1 | 5 | 5 | | | 3 | 3 | 4 | | | | | |

Can you write a number sentence (equation) that shows the relationship of the shorter sides to the longer side of a triangle?

_____

How many triangles can you find in the patterns?

17

PIECES AND PATTERNS

# Trying Triangles

Name _____

Given these 56 possible outcomes when rolling 3 dice, label those that form a triangle.

| | | | | | | | | | | | | |
|---|---|---|---|---|---|---|---|---|---|---|---|---|
| 1 | 1 | 1 | yes | | 1 | 5 | 6 | no | | 3 | 3 | 5 | yes |
| 1 | 1 | 2 | no | | 1 | 6 | 6 | yes | | 3 | 3 | 6 | no |
| 1 | 1 | 3 | no | | 2 | 2 | 2 | yes | | 3 | 4 | 4 | yes |
| 1 | 1 | 4 | no | | 2 | 2 | 3 | yes | | 3 | 4 | 5 | yes |
| 1 | 1 | 5 | no | | 2 | 2 | 4 | no | | 3 | 4 | 6 | yes |
| 1 | 1 | 6 | no | | 2 | 2 | 5 | no | | 3 | 5 | 5 | yes |
| 1 | 2 | 2 | yes | | 2 | 2 | 6 | no | | 3 | 5 | 6 | yes |
| 1 | 2 | 3 | no | | 2 | 3 | 3 | yes | | 3 | 6 | 6 | yes |
| 1 | 2 | 4 | no | | 2 | 3 | 4 | yes | | 4 | 4 | 4 | yes |
| 1 | 2 | 5 | no | | 2 | 3 | 5 | no | | 4 | 4 | 5 | yes |
| 1 | 2 | 6 | no | | 2 | 3 | 6 | no | | 4 | 4 | 6 | yes |
| 1 | 3 | 3 | yes | | 2 | 4 | 4 | yes | | 4 | 5 | 5 | yes |
| 1 | 3 | 4 | no | | 2 | 4 | 5 | yes | | 4 | 5 | 6 | yes |
| 1 | 3 | 5 | no | | 2 | 4 | 6 | no | | 4 | 6 | 6 | yes |
| 1 | 3 | 6 | no | | 2 | 5 | 5 | yes | | 5 | 5 | 5 | yes |
| 1 | 4 | 4 | yes | | 2 | 5 | 6 | yes | | 5 | 5 | 6 | yes |
| 1 | 4 | 5 | no | | 2 | 6 | 6 | yes | | 5 | 6 | 6 | yes |
| 1 | 4 | 6 | no | | 3 | 3 | 3 | yes | | 6 | 6 | 6 | yes |
| 1 | 5 | 5 | yes | | 3 | 3 | 4 | yes | | | | | |

Can you write a number sentence (equation) that shows the relationship of the shorter sides to the longer side of a triangle?

$$a + b > c$$

How many triangles can you find in the patterns?

18

PIECES AND PATTERNS

# See How They Roll

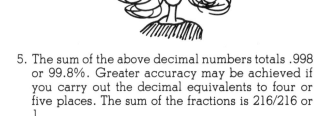

## I. Topic Area
Probability and Statistics

## II. Introductory Statement
Students will explore the probability of rolling three dice so that a given type of triangle will result.

## III. Math Skills
a. Classifying triangles by sides
b. Geometry
c. Fractions
d. Decimals
e. Probability

### Science Processes
a. Observing and classifying
b. Recording data
c. Predicting
d. Interpreting data
e. Applying and generalizing

## IV. Materials
Chart of possible outcomes that form a triangle from *Trying Triangles*.

## V. Key Question
What is the probability of forming an equilateral triangle? an isosceles triangle? a scalene triangle? no triangle?

## VI. Educative Input
1. One must recognize the difference between theoretical and experimental probability. In theoretical probability, all the possible arrangements must be considered. Experimentally, all the possible arrangements may not appear.
2. There are 216 possible arrangements of numbers when rolling three dice. Of these only 111 will result in the formation of a triangle.
3. When discussing probability you may wish to guide students to discovering that there are four possible kinds of outcomes that may occur when rolling three dice: (1) an equilateral triangle, (2) an isosceles triangle, (3) a scalene triangle, or (4) no triangle.
4. Let P = probability and E, I, and S represent equilateral, isosceles, and scalene triangles respectively. Z may represent no triangle and T is the total number of possible outcomes when rolling three dice. (theoretical probability)

$$P(E) = \frac{6}{216} = .027 = 2.7\%$$

$$P(I) = \frac{63}{216} = .291 = 29.1\%$$

$$P(S) = \frac{42}{216} = .194 = 19.4\%$$

$$P(Z) = \frac{105}{216} = .486 = 48.6\%$$

5. The sum of the above decimal numbers totals .998 or 99.8%. Greater accuracy may be achieved if you carry out the decimal equivalents to four or five places. The sum of the fractions is 216/216 or 1.

## VIII. Prodecure
1. Distribute the worksheet See How They Roll.
2. Classify the combinations of numbers according to the type of triangle formed.
3. Analyze the data by expressing the results in terms of probability.
4. Test results and express as a fraction, a decimal, and a percent.

## IX. What the Students Will Do
1. Classify triangles by type.
2. Analyze data by expressing results in terms of probability.
3. Express results as a fraction, a decimal, and a percent.
4. Test results by rolling dice and comparing results to expectations. (Experimental probability)

## X. Discussion
1. What is the probability of rolling three dice and being able to construct a triangle? (just over half, .512).
2. Which type of triangle is most likely to occur? (isosceles, .291). Least likely? (equilateral, .027). Why? (The probability of rolling three numbers the same is less than two numbers the same or no numbers the same.)
3. How often is it likely to happen that a triangle will not result from a given roll of three dice? (slightly less than half, .486).
4. What other kinds of chance events can we explore? (coin toss, colored spinner, or other number cubes.)

## IX. Extension
1. See *Probably Pythagorean*.

**PIECES AND PATTERNS**

# SEE HOW THEY ROLL

NAME _____

These combinations of numbers result in the construction of a Triangle. (111).

Classify each according to the type of triangle.

E for equilateral (all sides equal)
I for isosceles (two sides equal)
S for scalene (no sides equal)

| | | | | |
|---|---|---|---|---|
| 1 1 1 __ | 2 6 5 __ | 3 5 6 __ | 4 5 2 __ | 5 4 3 __ | 6 3 4 __ |
| 1 2 2 __ | 2 6 6 __ | 3 6 4 __ | 4 5 3 __ | 5 4 4 __ | 6 3 5 __ |
| 1 3 3 __ | 3 1 3 __ | 3 6 5 __ | 4 5 4 __ | 5 4 5 __ | 6 3 6 __ |
| 1 4 4 __ | 3 2 2 __ | 3 6 6 __ | 4 5 5 __ | 5 4 6 __ | 6 4 3 __ |
| 1 5 5 __ | 3 2 3 __ | 4 1 4 __ | 4 5 6 __ | 5 5 1 __ | 6 4 4 __ |
| 1 6 6 __ | 3 2 4 __ | 4 2 3 __ | 4 6 3 __ | 5 5 2 __ | 6 4 5 __ |
| 2 1 2 __ | 3 3 1 __ | 4 2 4 __ | 4 6 4 __ | 5 5 3 __ | 6 4 6 __ |
| 2 2 1 __ | 3 3 2 __ | 4 2 5 __ | 4 6 5 __ | 5 5 4 __ | 6 5 2 __ |
| 2 2 2 __ | 3 3 3 __ | 4 3 2 __ | 4 6 6 __ | 5 5 5 __ | 6 5 3 __ |
| 2 2 3 __ | 3 3 4 __ | 4 3 3 __ | 5 1 5 __ | 5 5 6 __ | 6 5 4 __ |
| 2 3 2 __ | 3 3 5 __ | 4 3 4 __ | 5 2 4 __ | 5 6 2 __ | 6 5 5 __ |
| 2 3 3 __ | 3 4 2 __ | 4 3 5 __ | 5 2 5 __ | 5 6 3 __ | 6 5 6 __ |
| 2 3 4 __ | 3 4 3 __ | 4 3 6 __ | 5 2 6 __ | 5 6 4 __ | 6 6 1 __ |
| 2 4 3 __ | 3 4 4 __ | 4 4 1 __ | 5 3 3 __ | 5 6 5 __ | 6 6 2 __ |
| 2 4 4 __ | 3 4 5 __ | 4 4 2 __ | 5 3 4 __ | 5 6 6 __ | 6 6 3 __ |
| 2 4 5 __ | 3 4 6 __ | 4 4 3 __ | 5 3 5 __ | 6 1 6 __ | 6 6 4 __ |
| 2 5 4 __ | 3 5 3 __ | 4 4 4 __ | 5 3 6 __ | 6 2 5 __ | 6 6 5 __ |
| 2 5 5 __ | 3 5 4 __ | 4 4 5 __ | 5 4 2 __ | 6 2 6 __ | 6 6 6 __ |
| 2 5 6 __ | 3 5 5 __ | 4 4 6 __ | | | |

Summarize the data into a Table:

| Type of Triangle | Total Number |
|---|---|
| EQUILATERAL | |
| ISOSCELES | |
| SCALENE | |
| TOTAL | |

20

PIECES AND PATTERNS

# SEE HOW THEY ROLL

NAME

These combinations of numbers result in the construction of a Triangle. (III).

Classify each according to the type of triangle.

E for equilateral (all sides equal)
I for isosceles (two sides equal)
S for scalene (no sides equal)

| | | | | | |
|---|---|---|---|---|---|
| 1 1 1 E | 2 6 5 S | 3 5 6 S | 4 5 2 S | 5 4 3 S | 6 3 4 S |
| 1 2 2 I | 2 6 6 I | 3 6 4 S | 4 5 3 S | 5 4 4 I | 6 3 5 S |
| 1 3 3 I | 3 1 3 I | 3 6 5 S | 4 5 4 I | 5 4 5 I | 6 3 6 I |
| 1 4 4 I | 3 2 2 I | 3 6 6 I | 4 5 5 I | 5 4 6 S | 6 4 3 S |
| 1 5 5 I | 3 2 3 I | 4 1 4 I | 4 5 6 S | 5 5 1 I | 6 4 4 I |
| 1 6 6 I | 3 2 4 S | 4 2 3 S | 4 6 3 S | 5 5 2 I | 6 4 5 S |
| 2 1 2 I | 3 3 1 I | 4 2 4 I | 4 6 4 I | 5 5 3 I | 6 4 6 I |
| 2 2 1 I | 3 3 2 I | 4 2 5 S | 4 6 5 S | 5 5 4 I | 6 5 2 S |
| 2 2 2 E | 3 3 3 E | 4 3 2 S | 4 6 6 I | 5 5 5 E | 6 5 3 S |
| 2 2 3 I | 3 3 4 I | 4 3 3 I | 5 1 5 I | 5 5 6 I | 6 5 4 S |
| 2 3 2 I | 3 3 5 I | 4 3 4 I | 5 2 4 S | 5 6 2 S | 6 5 5 I |
| 2 3 3 I | 3 4 2 S | 4 3 5 S | 5 2 5 I | 5 6 3 S | 6 5 6 I |
| 2 3 4 S | 3 4 3 I | 4 3 6 S | 5 2 6 S | 5 6 4 S | 6 6 1 I |
| 2 4 3 S | 3 4 4 I | 4 4 1 I | 5 3 3 I | 5 6 5 I | 6 6 2 I |
| 2 4 4 I | 3 4 5 S | 4 4 2 I | 5 3 4 S | 5 6 6 I | 6 6 3 I |
| 2 4 5 S | 3 4 6 S | 4 4 3 I | 5 3 5 I | 6 1 6 I | 6 6 4 I |
| 2 5 4 S | 3 5 3 I | 4 4 4 E | 5 3 6 S | 6 2 5 S | 6 6 5 I |
| 2 5 5 I | 3 5 4 S | 4 4 5 I | 5 4 2 S | 6 2 6 I | 6 6 6 E |
| 2 5 6 S | 3 5 5 I | 4 4 6 I | | | |

Summarize the data into a Table:

| Type of Triangle | | Total Number |
|---|---|---|
| EQUILATERAL | | 6 |
| ISOSCELES | | 63 |
| SCALENE | | 42 |
| | TOTAL | 111 |

21

PIECES AND PATTERNS

# SEE HOW THEY ROLL

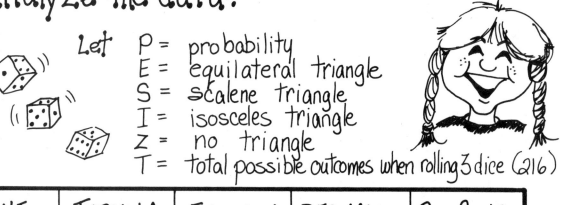

## A. Analyze the data:

Let  P = probability
     E = equilateral triangle
     S = scalene triangle
     I = isosceles triangle
     Z = no triangle
     T = total possible outcomes when rolling 3 dice (216)

| EVENT | FORMULA | FRACTION | DECIMAL | PER CENT |
|-------|---------|----------|---------|----------|
| P(E)  | $\frac{E}{T}$ | | | |
| P(I)  | $\frac{I}{T}$ | | | |
| P(S)  | $\frac{S}{T}$ | | | |
| P(Z)  | $\frac{Z}{T}$ | | | |

## B. Testing the results:

Roll the dice 25 times, then 50 times. Record.

| $\frac{n}{25}$ | E | | | I | | | S | | | Z | | | 25 ROLLS |
|------|----------|---------|----------|----------|---------|----------|----------|---------|----------|----------|---------|----------|---|
| | fraction | decimal | per cent | fraction | decimal | per cent | fraction | decimal | per cent | fraction | decimal | per cent | |
| | | | | | | | | | | | | | |

| $\frac{n}{50}$ | E | | | I | | | S | | | Z | | | 50 ROLLS |
|------|----------|---------|----------|----------|---------|----------|----------|---------|----------|----------|---------|----------|---|
| | fraction | decimal | per cent | fraction | decimal | per cent | fraction | decimal | per cent | fraction | decimal | per cent | |
| | | | | | | | | | | | | | |

## C. How do these results compare with your expectations? _____

_____

_____

22

# SEE HOW THEY ROLL

## A. Analyze the data:

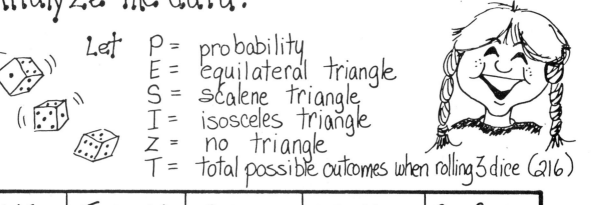

Let
- P = probability
- E = equilateral triangle
- S = scalene triangle
- I = isosceles triangle
- Z = no triangle
- T = total possible outcomes when rolling 3 dice (216)

| EVENT | FORMULA | FRACTION | DECIMAL | PER CENT |
|-------|---------|----------|---------|----------|
| P(E) | $\frac{E}{T}$ | $\frac{6}{216}$ | $.02\bar{7}$ | 2.7 % |
| P(I) | $\frac{I}{T}$ | $\frac{63}{216}$ | .291 | 29.1 % |
| P(S) | $\frac{S}{T}$ | $\frac{42}{216}$ | $.19\bar{4}$ | 19.4 % |
| P(Z) | $\frac{Z}{T}$ | $\frac{105}{216}$ | .486 | 48.6 % |

## B. Testing the results:
Roll the dice 25 times, then 50 times. Record.

| $\frac{n}{25}$ | E | | | I | | | S | | | Z | | | 25 ROLLS |
|------|----------|---------|----------|----------|---------|----------|----------|---------|----------|----------|---------|----------|---|
| | fraction | decimal | per cent | fraction | decimal | per cent | fraction | decimal | per cent | fraction | decimal | per cent | |
| | | | | | | | | | | | | | |

| $\frac{n}{50}$ | E | | | I | | | S | | | Z | | | 50 ROLLS |
|------|----------|---------|----------|----------|---------|----------|----------|---------|----------|----------|---------|----------|---|
| | fraction | decimal | per cent | fraction | decimal | per cent | fraction | decimal | per cent | fraction | decimal | per cent | |
| | | | | | | | | | | | | | |

## C. How do these results compare with your expectations? _____

_____

23

PIECES AND PATTERNS

## I. Topic Area
Probability and statistics

## II. Introductory Statement
Students will determine what the probability will be that the resulting triangles will be acute, obtuse, or right triangles by applying the Pythagorean theory.

## III. Math Skills
a. Geometry
b. Algebra
c. Problem solving
d. Applying formulas
e. Equalities and inequalities
f. Pythagorean Theorem

### Science Processes
a. Classifying
b. Predicting
c. Interpreting data
d. Generalizing

## IV. Materials
Chart from *See How They Roll* of numbers generated from rolling three dice that result in the construction of a triangle.

## V. Key Question
Can you determine which of the resulting triangles will be acute, obtuse or right?

## VI. Educative Input
1. The Pythagorean Theorem states that in a right triangle the sum of the squares of the legs is equal to the square of the hypotenuse.

$$a^2 + b^2 = c^2$$

2. Therefore we can say that if the sum of the squares of the shorter sides of a triangle is equal to the square of the longer side, the triangle is a right triangle.

3. Further, if the sum of the squares of the two shorter sides is greater than the square of the longest side, the triangle is an acute triangle.

$$a^2 + b^2 > c^2$$

4. And if the sum of the squares of the two short sides is less than the square of the longest side, the triangle is obtuse.

$$a^2 + b^2 < c^2$$

5. Of the 216 possible outcomes, there are 56 unique combinations of numbers (no repeated arrangements). Of those 56 combinations only 34 will form a triangle. For this reason, only 34 combinations are entered in the table and one must remember to multiply by the number of arrangements of each combination of numbers.

## VII. Management Suggestions
1. Students may work in pairs or independently to apply the formulas.
2. When testing results it is best to work in pairs.

## VIII. Procedure
1. Students will classify each of the resulting triangles according to the type of angle using this notation:
   R = Right triangle
   A = Acute triangle
   O = Obtuse triangle
2. Analyze results by expressing in terms of probability.
3. Express results as a fraction, a decimal, and a percent.
4. Test results by rolling dice and recording outcomes.
5. Compare with expected results.

## IX. What the Students Will Do
1. Classify triangles by type of angle.
2. Analyze data by expressing in terms of probability
3. Test results and compare data generated to expected results.

## X. Discussion
1. What is the probability of a right triangle occurring?

$$P(R) = \frac{\text{Number of R}}{\text{Total number of Possible Outcomes}}$$

$$P(R) = \frac{6}{216} = .02\overline{7} = 2.7\%$$

2. What is the probability of an acute triangle occurring?

$$P(A) = \frac{\text{Number of A}}{\text{Total number of Possible Outcomes}}$$

$$P(A) = \frac{66}{216} = .30\overline{5} = 30.6\%$$

3. What is the probability of an obtuse triangle occurring?

$$P(O) = \frac{\text{Number of O}}{\text{Total number of Possible Outcomes}}$$

$$P(O) = \frac{39}{216} = .180\overline{5} = 18.1\%$$

4. What is the probability of no triangles occurring?

$$P(Z) = \frac{\text{Number of Z}}{\text{Total number of Possible Outcomes}}$$

$$P(Z) = \frac{105}{216} = .486 = 48.6\%$$

## XI. Extension
1. We have examined the resulting triangles formed by using three dice with a total of 216 outcomes. Try using three spinners (1-8) or (1-12) and determine the total number of outcomes of each type.

# Probably Pythagorean!

Name _____

✳ Number of Arrangements

| SIDE A | SIDE B | SIDE C | A² | B² | ≤ C² | Type of Triangle | ✳ | | SIDE A | SIDE B | SIDE C | A² | B² | ≤ C² | Type of Triangle | ✳ |
|---|---|---|---|---|---|---|---|---|---|---|---|---|---|---|---|---|
| 1 | 1 | 1 | | | | | 1 | | 3 | 4 | 4 | | | | | 3 |
| 1 | 2 | 2 | | | | | 3 | | 3 | 4 | 5 | | | | | 6 |
| 1 | 3 | 3 | | | | | 3 | | 3 | 4 | 6 | | | | | 6 |
| 1 | 4 | 4 | | | | | 3 | | 3 | 5 | 5 | | | | | 3 |
| 1 | 5 | 5 | | | | | 3 | | 3 | 5 | 6 | | | | | 6 |
| 1 | 6 | 6 | | | | | 3 | | 3 | 6 | 6 | | | | | 3 |
| 2 | 2 | 2 | | | | | 1 | | 4 | 4 | 4 | | | | | 1 |
| 2 | 2 | 3 | | | | | 3 | | 4 | 4 | 5 | | | | | 3 |
| 2 | 3 | 3 | | | | | 3 | | 4 | 4 | 6 | | | | | 3 |
| 2 | 3 | 4 | | | | | 6 | | 4 | 5 | 5 | | | | | 3 |
| 2 | 4 | 4 | | | | | 3 | | 4 | 5 | 6 | | | | | 6 |
| 2 | 4 | 5 | | | | | 6 | | 4 | 6 | 6 | | | | | 3 |
| 2 | 5 | 5 | | | | | 3 | | 5 | 5 | 5 | | | | | 1 |
| 2 | 5 | 6 | | | | | 6 | | 5 | 5 | 6 | | | | | 3 |
| 2 | 6 | 6 | | | | | 3 | | 5 | 6 | 6 | | | | | 3 |
| 3 | 3 | 3 | | | | | 1 | | 6 | 6 | 6 | | | | | 1 |
| 3 | 3 | 4 | | | | | 3 | | | | | | | | | |
| 3 | 3 | 5 | | | | | 3 | | | | | | | | | |

Classify according to the type of triangle:

R for Right $(a^2 + b^2 = c^2)$
A for Acute $(a^2 + b^2 > c^2)$
O for Obtuse $(a^2 + b^2 < c^2)$

Now:
Summarize the data into a table:

| Type of Triangle | Total Number |
|---|---|
| RIGHT | |
| ACUTE | |
| OBTUSE | |
| Total | |

Pythagorean Problems

PIECES AND PATTERNS

# Probably Pythagorean!

| SIDE A | SIDE B | SIDE C | A² | B² | (A²+B²) ⋛ C² | C² | Type of Triangle | * |
|---|---|---|---|---|---|---|---|---|
| 1 | 1 | 1 | 1 | 1 | > | 1 | A | 1 |
| 1 | 2 | 2 | 1 | 4 | > | 4 | A | 3 |
| 1 | 3 | 3 | 1 | 9 | > | 9 | A | 3 |
| 1 | 4 | 4 | 1 | 16 | > | 16 | A | 3 |
| 1 | 5 | 5 | 1 | 25 | > | 25 | A | 3 |
| 1 | 6 | 6 | 1 | 36 | > | 36 | A | 3 |
| 2 | 2 | 2 | 4 | 4 | > | 4 | A | 1 |
| 2 | 2 | 3 | 4 | 4 | < | 9 | O | 3 |
| 2 | 3 | 3 | 4 | 9 | > | 9 | A | 3 |
| 2 | 3 | 4 | 4 | 9 | < | 16 | O | 6 |
| 2 | 4 | 4 | 4 | 16 | > | 16 | A | 3 |
| 2 | 4 | 5 | 4 | 16 | < | 25 | O | 6 |
| 2 | 5 | 5 | 4 | 25 | > | 25 | A | 3 |
| 2 | 5 | 6 | 4 | 25 | < | 36 | O | 6 |
| 2 | 6 | 6 | 4 | 36 | > | 36 | A | 3 |
| 3 | 3 | 3 | 9 | 9 | > | 9 | A | 1 |
| 3 | 3 | 4 | 9 | 9 | > | 16 | A | 3 |
| 3 | 3 | 5 | 9 | 9 | < | 25 | O | 3 |
| 3 | 4 | 4 | 9 | 16 | > | 16 | A | 3 |
| 3 | 4 | 5 | 9 | 16 | = | 25 | R | 6 |
| 3 | 4 | 6 | 9 | 16 | < | 36 | O | 6 |
| 3 | 5 | 5 | 9 | 25 | > | 25 | A | 3 |
| 3 | 5 | 6 | 9 | 25 | < | 36 | O | 6 |
| 3 | 6 | 6 | 9 | 36 | > | 36 | A | 3 |
| 4 | 4 | 4 | 16 | 16 | > | 16 | A | 1 |
| 4 | 4 | 5 | 16 | 16 | > | 25 | A | 3 |
| 4 | 4 | 6 | 16 | 16 | < | 36 | O | 3 |
| 4 | 5 | 5 | 16 | 25 | > | 25 | A | 3 |
| 4 | 5 | 6 | 16 | 25 | > | 36 | A | 6 |
| 4 | 6 | 6 | 16 | 36 | > | 36 | A | 3 |
| 5 | 5 | 5 | 25 | 25 | > | 25 | A | 1 |
| 5 | 5 | 6 | 25 | 25 | > | 36 | A | 3 |
| 5 | 6 | 6 | 25 | 36 | > | 36 | A | 3 |
| 6 | 6 | 6 | 36 | 36 | > | 36 | A | 1 |

\* Number of Arrangements

Classify according to the type of triangle:

R for Right ($a^2 + b^2 = c^2$)
A for Acute ($a^2 + b^2 > c^2$)
O for Obtuse ($a^2 + b^2 < c^2$)

Now: Summarize the data into a table:

| Type of Triangle | Total Number |
|---|---|
| RIGHT | 6 |
| ACUTE | 66 |
| OBTUSE | 39 |
| Total | 111 |

(Pythagorean Problems)

PIECES AND PATTERNS

)

# Probably Pythagorean!

## A. Analyze the data:

Let
- P = probability
- R = right triangle
- A = acute triangle
- O = obtuse triangle
- Z = no triangle
- T = total possible outcomes when rolling 3 dice (216)

| EVENT | FORMULA | FRACTION | DECIMAL | PER CENT % |
|-------|---------|----------|---------|------------|
| P(R) | $\frac{R}{T}$ | | | |
| P(A) | $\frac{A}{T}$ | | | |
| P(O) | $\frac{O}{T}$ | | | |
| P(Z) | $\frac{Z}{T}$ | | | |

## B. Testing the results:

Roll the dice 25 times, then 50 times. Record.

| $\frac{n}{25}$ | R | | | A | | | O | | | Z | | | 25 Rolls |
|------|----------|---------|---------|----------|---------|---------|----------|---------|---------|----------|---------|----------|------|
| | fraction | decimal | percent | fraction | decimal | percent | fraction | decimal | percent | fraction | decimal | per cent | |
| | | | | | | | | | | | | | |

| $\frac{n}{50}$ | R | | | A | | | O | | | Z | | | 50 Rolls |
|------|----------|---------|---------|----------|---------|---------|----------|---------|---------|----------|---------|----------|------|
| | fraction | decimal | per cent | fraction | decimal | per cent | fraction | decimal | percent | fraction | decimal | percent | |
| | | | | | | | | | | | | | |

## C. How do these results compare with your expectations?

_____

_____

**PIECES AND PATTERNS**

# Probably Pythagorean!

## A. Analyze the data:

Let  P = probability
     R = right triangle
     A = acute triangle
     O = obtuse triangle
     Z = no triangle
     T = total possible outcomes when rolling 3 dice (216)

| EVENT | FORMULA | FRACTION | DECIMAL | PER CENT % |
|-------|---------|----------|---------|------------|
| P(R) | $\frac{R}{T}$ | $\frac{6}{216}$ | $.02\overline{7}$ | 2.7 |
| P(A) | $\frac{A}{T}$ | $\frac{66}{216}$ | $.30\overline{5}$ | 30.6 |
| P(O) | $\frac{O}{T}$ | $\frac{39}{216}$ | $.180\overline{5}$ | 18.1 |
| P(Z) | $\frac{Z}{T}$ | $\frac{105}{216}$ | $.486$ | 48.6 |

## B. Testing the results:

Roll the dice 25 times, then 50 times. Record.

| $\frac{n}{25}$ | R | | | A | | | O | | | Z | | | 25 Rolls |
|---|---|---|---|---|---|---|---|---|---|---|---|---|---|
| | fraction | decimal | percent | fraction | decimal | percent | fraction | decimal | percent | fraction | decimal | per cent | |
| | | | | | | | | | | | | | |

| $\frac{n}{50}$ | R | | | A | | | O | | | Z | | | 50 Rolls |
|---|---|---|---|---|---|---|---|---|---|---|---|---|---|
| | fraction | decimal | percent | fraction | decimal | percent | fraction | decimal | percent | fraction | decimal | percent | |
| | | | | | | | | | | | | | |

## C. How do these results compare with your expectations?

_____

PIECES AND PATTERNS

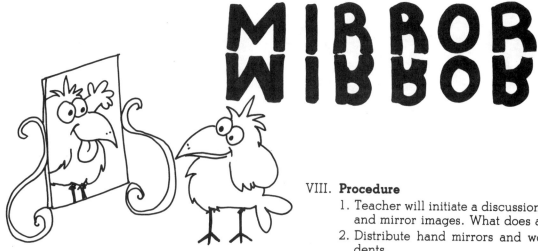

# MIRROR MIRROR

## I. Topic Area
Mirrors and Symmetry

## II. Introductory Statement
Students will use a hand mirror to explore mirror images of alphabet letters.

## III. Math Skills
a. Geometry
b. Symmetry
c. Logic
d. Patterns
e. Spatial relationships

## Science Processes
a. Observing and classifying
b. Predicting
c. Comparing
d. Organizing data
e. Generalizing information

## IV. Materials
Hand mirror for each student

## V. Key Question
What does a mirror do? Which letters of the alphabet will look exactly like their mirror image?

## VI. Educative Input
1. A mirror is simply a piece of glass with a backing of silver and paint.
2. Letters or numbers that have no directionality will appear the same as their mirror image. For example, the letter A has no "direction"; whereas the letter B must appear with the "loops" on the right. Perhaps some students will "see" it better if you talk about the front and the back of a letter being the same to produce an identical mirror image. Some letters simply appear backwards in the mirror.

## VII. Management Suggestions
1. Students may wish to work independently or in partners.
2. Remind students that mirrors are easily broken and when not in use should be placed in a protective covering in a safe place.
3. Indicate to students that it will be easier to copy the letter image in the mirror if you place the mirror on the left side of the letter if you are right-handed and on the right side if you are left-handed.

## VIII. Procedure
1. Teacher will initiate a discussion about reflection and mirror images. What does a mirror do?
2. Distribute hand mirrors and worksheets to students.
3. Students will first of all predict which letters of the alphabet and which numbers 0-9 will appear the same in the mirror as they do on paper by placing a check (✔) beneath each letter or number.
4. Students will then use a hand mirror and place it to the right or left side of each letter and number, and copy in the space beneath, the image that appears in the mirror.
5. Count and record the number of symbols that appear identical to their mirror image.
6. Describe how the letters that are identical in the mirror are different from the letters that do *not* appear the same in the mirror.
7. Can you generalize why some alphabet letters are exactly like their mirror image and others are not?

## IX. What the Students Will Do
1. Students will predict which letters and numbers will appear the same as their mirror image.
2. Students will use a hand mirror to copy the mirror image of each letter and number.
3. Students will count and record the number of symbols that are identical to their mirror image.
4. Students will generalize why some letters are identical to their mirror image and others are not.
5. Students will create word and number palindromes and predict and record their mirror images.

## X. Discussion
1. What does a mirror do?
2. What is a mirror image?
3. Why do some ambulances have "ambulance" written backwards across the front of the car? (So that it can be read in the rear view mirror from another vehicle.)
4. Name some ways mirrors are helpful to people. (dentists, department and clothing stores, beauty shops, haunted houses, home decorating, bathrooms, etc.)

## XI. Extensions
1. See *Halves and Halve Nots.* Explore mirrors and lines of symmetry.

# MIRROR

Please √ the letters and numbers that you think will appear the same in the mirror as they do on this paper.

| Letter | A | B | C | D | E | F | G | H | I | J | K | L | M | N | O | P |
|---|---|---|---|---|---|---|---|---|---|---|---|---|---|---|---|---|
| √ here | | | | | | | | | | | | | | | | |
| mirror view | | | | | | | | | | | | | | | | |

| Letter | Q | R | S | T | U | V | W | X | Y | Z |
|---|---|---|---|---|---|---|---|---|---|---|
| √ here | | | | | | | | | | |
| mirror view | | | | | | | | | | |

| Number | 0 | 1 | 2 | 3 | 4 | 5 | 6 | 7 | 8 | 9 |
|---|---|---|---|---|---|---|---|---|---|---|
| √ here | | | | | | | | | | |
| mirror view | | | | | | | | | | |

Now, place the mirror to the right or left side of each letter or number and beneath each one, copy what you see in the mirror.

How many letters and numbers appear the same in the mirror? _____

Describe how the letters and numbers that look exactly like their mirror image are different from letters that do not appear like their mirror image.

_____

_____

Write a generalization that explains why some alphabet letters are exactly like their mirror image. _____

_____

PIECES AND PATTERNS

# MIRROR PALINDROMES

_____
NAME

Some words read the same forward as they do backward They are called palindromes. Do they look the same in the mirror?

Predict whether or not the mirror image is identical then use a mirror to copy and record the mirror image.

| Palindrome | Prediction | Mirror Image |
|---|---|---|
| 1. MOM | 1. | 1. |
| 2. DAD | 2. | 2. |
| 3. | 3. | 3. |
| 4. | 4. | 4. |
| 5. | 5. | 5. |

*create 3 more of your own*

Some numbers read the same forward as they do backward. They also are called palindromes. Do they look the same as their mirror image? Hint: Which digits are the only ones that look like their mirror image?

Predict whether or not they are the same as their mirror image. Use the mirror to copy the image.

| Palindrome | Prediction | Mirror Image |
|---|---|---|
| 1. | 1. | 1. |
| 2. | 2. | 2. |
| 3. | 3. | 3. |
| 4. | 4. | 4. |
| 5. | 5. | 5. |

*Find and record 5 Number Palindromes*

# Halves and Halve-nots

## I. Topic Area
Mirrors and symmetry

## II. Introductory Statement
Students will use hand mirrors to discover lines of symmetry in letters of the alphabet.

## III. Math Skills / Science Processes

| Math Skills | Science Processes |
|---|---|
| a. Geometry | a. Observing |
| b. Patterns | b. Classifying |
| c. Symmetry | c. Predicting |
| d. Logic | d. Comparing |
| e. Spatial relationships | e. Interpreting data |
| | f. Generalizing |

## IV. Materials
Hand mirrors
Fine tipped colored pen or pencil

## V. Key Question
What letter of the alphabet has the most lines of symmetry? Why?

## VI. Educative Input
1. When a line can be drawn through an object to produce identical parts, we say it has bilateral symmetry. You may wish to illustrate by asking what will happen if you draw half a man and then hold a mirror down the middle of him. You get an identical half which makes him a whole man. This line is called a line of symmetry. Sometimes people call them balance lines.
2. Some figures have no lines of symmetry; while others have many.

## VII. Management Suggestions
1. Students may work in pairs but each will have his own recording sheet.
2. *Halve a Code* could be used as a homework assignment.

## VIII. Procedure
1. Define and demonstrate lines of symmetry.
2. Distribute worksheets and hand mirrors.
3. Use a hand mirror to find lines of symmetry in objects pictured at top of worksheet. Record by using colored pen or pencil to draw a dotted line to show path of each line of symmetry.
4. Teacher will stop at this point for brief discussion and clarification (if necessary) of sample objects.
5. Predict how many letters will have at least one line of symmetry.
6. Use mirrors to find the lines of symmetry in each letter of the alphabet. Draw in dotted lines with colored pen or pencil to show path of lines of symmetry. Record the number of symmetry lines in each letter.
7. Organize and display the data generated in the table provided.

## IX. What the Students Will Do
1. Use mirrors to find the lines of symmetry in familiar objects and letters.
2. Draw lines of symmetry.
3. Count and record the number of lines of symmetry.
4. Organize and analyze the data generated into a table.
5. Apply knowledge of lines of symmetry in alphabet letters to encode a message using "half" letters. Trade codes with a friend and decode the message.

## X. Discussion
1. What is a line of symmetry?
2. What words can we use to describe the "direction" of lines of symmetry? (vertical symmetry, horizontal symmetry, diagonal symmetry.)
3. What shapes produce the most lines of symmetry? the least?
4. Name or list things in your environment that have symmetry—in nature or man-made.

## XI. Extensions
1. See *Nature's Part in Art and Math* for extensions of three kinds of symmetry: bilateral, translational and rotational.

32

# Halves and Halve-nots

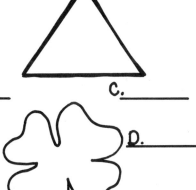

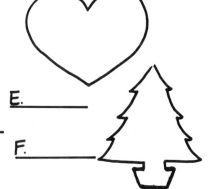

B. _____   C. _____   E. _____   D. _____   F. _____   A. _____

Use your mirror to find
a line or lines of symmetry in each picture. Draw in the line or
lines of symmetry with a colored pen. (Use dotted lines)

---

How Many Alphabet Letters have one or more lines of symmetry?
I predict _____ letters have lines of symmetry....

Circle the correct answer:

$\frac{1}{2}$ of 8 =

○ 0
● 3
○ 4

| Show lines of Symmetry | A | B | C | D | E | F | G | H | I | J | K | L | M |
|---|---|---|---|---|---|---|---|---|---|---|---|---|---|
| | Ä | B̶ | | | | | | | | | | | |
| how many | 1 | 1 | | | | | | | | | | | |

| Show lines of Symmetry | N | O | P | Q | R | S | T | U | V | W | X | Y | Z |
|---|---|---|---|---|---|---|---|---|---|---|---|---|---|
| | | | | | | | | | | | | | |
| how many? | | | | | | | | | | | | | |

| Number of lines of symmetry | Alphabet letters (list them) |
|---|---|
| 0 | |
| 1 | |
| 2 | |
| 3 | |
| 4 | |
| more than 4 | |
| Total 26 | |

Complete this table

33

PIECES AND PATTERNS

# Halve a Code

ENCODER_____
DECODER_____

Devise a secret code using lines of symmetry of letters. Record a message here by writing only alphabet "halves". For instance, A could be written ⅄ or ⅄. For letters with no lines of symmetry, you could write the complete letter. To make it more difficult, you may simply leave a blank space indicating that one of the letters with 0 lines of symmetry may be used there.

Trade with a partner and decode each other's message. You may use mirrors if you wish.

EXAMPLE

M  CODE        (MY CODE )

ENCODED  MESSAGE:

DECODED  MESSAGE:

34
PIECES AND PATTERNS

# Mirrors that Multiply

## I. Topic Area
Mirrors, multiple images and patterns

## II. Introductory Statement
Students will explore the principles of multiple images and reflections and apply them to the construction of a simple kaleidoscope.

## III. Math Skills
a. Measuring angles
b. Counting
c. Symmetry

### Science Processes
a. Observing
b. Predicting and inferring
c. Organizing data
d. Applying and generalizing

## IV. Materials
Mirrors—small hand mirrors or strips (1″×6″) of mirrored glass
Protractors

## V. Key Question
How can I use mirrors to multiply?

## VI. Educative Input
1. Images are made by light from a light source focused on a surface.
2. An image disappears when direct light from the object is blocked.
3. An image differs from an ordinary picture of an object because pictures can be seen even when the object is missing.
4. The term image is used here to describe the picture of an object one sees in a mirror.

## VII. Management Suggestions
1. Sheets of mirrored glass (approximately 8″×11″) may be purchased inexpensively at any K-Mart type store or hardware outlet. Cut large pieces with a glass cutter into desired lengths and tape the edges with masking tape for safety in handling.
2. Students may work well in teams of 2-3, depending upon the number of mirrors available.

## VIII. Procedure
1. Distribute mirrors: 2 per team, and worksheets.
2. Predict the total number of "stars" you think you will see when placing two mirrors facing one another on the sides of each given angle (include the object star).
3. Set mirrors upright on given line segments and measure the resulting angle. Record.
4. Count the total number of star images plus the star object and record.
5. Repeat for each new angle.
6. Analyze the data and form a conclusion showing the relationship between the size of the angle and the number of images reflected.
7. Apply this generalization to a pattern of shapes on worksheet...Krazy Kaleidoscope.
8. Create your own crazy pattern.
9. Join three mirrors together with a rubber band to form a triangular tube (a simple kaleidoscope).

## IX. What the Students Will Do
1. Predict the number of stars in the mirrors.
2. Measure angles and record the total number of stars counted at each angle.
3. Describe the relationship of size of angle to the number of stars.
4. Create a pattern to be "multiplied".
5. Make a primitive kaleidoscope.

## X. Discussion
1. As the angle between the mirrors becomes smaller, what happens to the number of images reflected?
2. Why were you able to count only 11 images at the 30° angle? How many did you expect to be able to count?
3. In applying what you've learned about multiple mirrors and images, how many mirrors do you think you need to produce an infinite number of images?
4. If you were to build a kaleidoscope within a circular tube, how many mirrors would you need to produce the greatest number of images?

## XI. Extensions
1. Build a kaleidoscope within a circular tube such as a potato chip can or a tennis ball can.

**PIECES AND PATTERNS**

# Mirrors that Multiply

Predict the total number of stars that you see at each angle.....Record in the table...

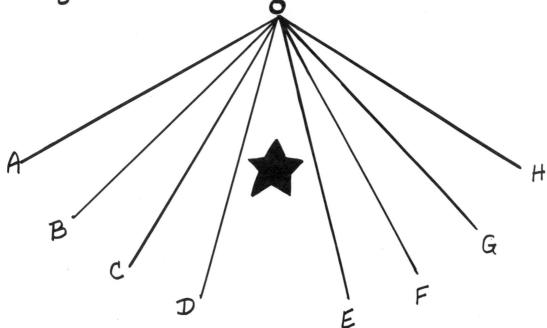

- Set 2 mirrors upright on line segment $\overline{AO}$ and line $\overline{HO}$ facing the center.
- Measure the angle. _____°.
- Count the total number of stars you see. _____.
- Move one mirror at a time; measure the ∠ and count the number of stars you see.
- Repeat until both mirrors are on lines $\overline{DO}$ and $\overline{EO}$.

Collect & Organize Data:

| Name of angle | No. of degrees | Predicted No. of Images | Actual No. of Images |
|---|---|---|---|
| ∠AOH | | | |
| ∠BOH | | | |
| ∠BOG | | | |
| ∠BOF | | | |
| ∠BOE | | | |
| ∠DOF | | | |
| ∠DOE | | | |

(circle one)

**Conclusion:** As the number of degrees in the angle becomes (less or greater) the number of images becomes (less or greater).

PIECES AND PATTERNS

# Krazy Kaleidoscope

• Decorate the design below with colors or patterns.
• Place mirrors on edges of this pattern and slowly converge mirrors toward each other.

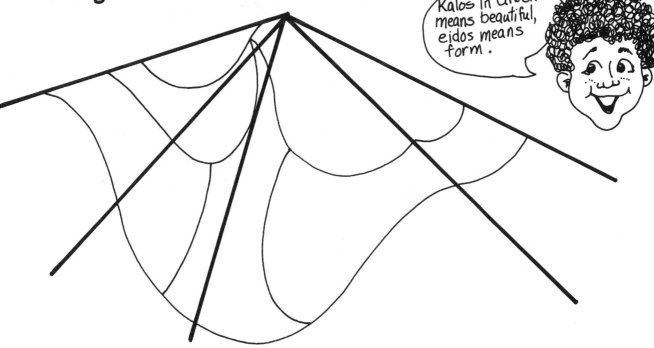

Kalos in Greek means beautiful, eidos means form.

• Write a metaphor or description of what you see : _____

_____

• Design a pattern of your own to share with a friend:

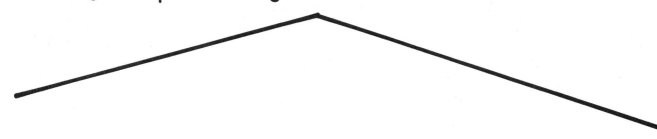

**PIECES AND PATTERNS**

# Do-It-Yourself Kaleidoscope

1. Tape the edges of 3 mirrors (size 6"x1")

2. Use a rubber band to join the mirrors together to form a triangular mirrored tube.

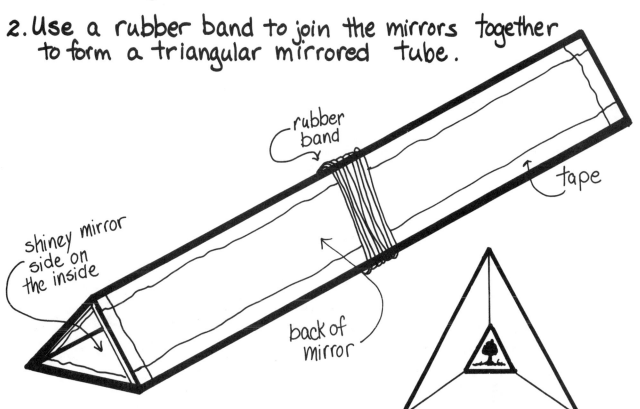

rubber band

tape

shiney mirror side on the inside

back of mirror

3. Look through one end and view your world . . . . one of reflected shapes and patterns.

38

PIECES AND PATTERNS

# THE NATURE OF SYMMETRY

## I. Topic Area
Symmetry and nature.

## II. Introductory Statement
Students will identify and explore three kinds of symmetry—bilateral, translational, and rotational—in our world of natural and man-made objects.

## III. Math Skills / Science Processes

**Math Skills**
a. Geometry
b. Symmetry
c. Spatial relationships
d. Patterns

**Science Processes**
a. Observing
b. Classifying
c. Interpreting data
d. Applying information
e. Generalizing

## IV. Materials
Construction paper
Card stock or index cards
Scissors
Glue
Colored pens or crayons

## V. Key Question
How can we identify and simulate patterns found in natural and man-made objects?

## VI. Educative Input
1. The world around us is filled with geometric order or balanced proportion called symmetry. We find it in flowers, animals, leaves, architecture, fabric, wallpaper, etc.
2. When one side (half) of an object matches the other side, we call this bilateral symmetry. By flipping one half onto the other, we can visualize its twin.
3. When we observe a repeated pattern in wallpaper or fabric, we find that an object has simply been moved up or down or to the side. This kind of order or symmetry is called translational.
4. If we observe a flower such as a daisy we can see the petals turn around the center of the flower. This kind of symmetry is called rotational symmetry. It can be achieved by turning a shape around a central point.

## VII. Management Suggestions
1. Do the activities to illustrate the types of symmetry as a total class experience.
2. Create a bulletin board where students can bring in samples or pictures that illustrate different kinds of symmetry.

## VIII. Procedure
1. Introduce the three kinds of symmetry by doing each of the activities described here.
   a. **Bilateral Symmetry:**
      Have students fold a piece of paper and write their names along the fold. Cut around the letters leaving the side along the fold attached. Open and mount on construction paper.
   b. **Translational Symmetry:**
      Fold a strip of paper in half lengthwise, then in half lengthwise again, and then once again lengthwise. Cut a figure or design into the center fold. Be sure to leave opposite side attached at one point. Cut away excess paper and open up. Four designs should be attached to one another. The shape has been repeated four times—an example of translational symmetry.
   c. **Rotational Symmetry:**
      Have students cut out of tagboard or index cards a simple shape and place it on a piece of construction paper. Thumbtack both to a cardboard placed under the construction paper. Trace around the shape; then rotate or turn it slightly and trace again. Repeat until the shape returns to its original position.
2. Make a list of natural and man-made examples of each kind of symmetry. Brainstorm ideas from all of the students.
3. Create a patchwork pattern by transferring and rotating a pattern of your own design.

## IX. What the Students Will Do
1. Observe and classify samples of three kinds of symmetry in natural and man-made objects.
2. Apply knowledge of symmetry to produce patchwork patterns by rotating a pattern.

## X. Discussion
1. Can we find examples of each kind of symmetry in the classroom? in our homes? outside?
2. How does symmetry help create a pattern? (It provides order and sequence.)
3. In addition and multiplication tables there is bilateral symmetry through the diagonal line. Can you discover why? (Inverse equations equal the same number: $4 + 2 = 2 + 4$.)

## XI. Extension
1. See *Nature's Part in Art and Math.*

# Nature's Part in Art...and Math

## I. Topic Area
Symmetry and shape in nature.

## II. Introductory Statement
Students will observe and identify major shapes (polygons) in natural objects and observe how they form patterns.

## III. Math Skills
a. Geometry
b. Patterns
c. Symmetry

### Science Processes
a. Observing
b. Interpreting data
c. Generalizing

## IV. Materials
spider web
honey comb
butterfly
flower

pine cone
leaf
sugar crystals
orange (cut crosswise)

## V. Key Question
How can we find and identify shapes and patterns in nature?

## VI. Educative Input
1. In science, all living things are structured in some form of symmetrical pattern. In math, the symmetry concept is essential to geometry. In art, balance, pattern and color are all parts of design symmetry.
2. Polygons (shapes) are closed figures formed by straight line segments. Straight line segments are referred to as sides. The point where two sides meet is called a vertex whose plural is vertices.
3. Tessellate or tiling means the repeated use of a polygon or shape to completely fill a region without gaps or overlap.

## VII. Management Suggestions
1. *Nature of Symmetry* introduces three kinds of symmetry and is a good pre-requisite.

## VIII. Procedure
1. Display as many "real" samples as possible from the materials list.
2. Observe and identify kinds of symmetry.
3. Observe and identify as many regular and irregular polygons as possible in "real" objects.
4. Distribute worksheets that simulate natural objects.
5. Have students identify and sketch major polygons they see, and the number of sides, angles and vertices and record.
6. (Optional) Using regular polygons, choose one nature pattern and create a similar one by tessellating or tiling one or more shapes on an 8" × 5" piece of construction paper.

## IX. What the Students Will Do
1. Observe and identify regular and irregular polygons in nature.
2. Observe and identify kinds of symmetry.
3. Identify and sketch major polygons (shapes) in simulated nature pictures.
4. Simulate a pattern in nature by tessellating regular polygons.

## X. Discussion
1. In a simple polygon, what is the relationship of sides, angles and vertices? (They are equal in number.)
2. How does the combination of shapes and symmetry create a pattern? (Shapes are the "what" you use and symmetry is the "how" or order you use.)

## XI. Extension
*Watch Crystals Grow*
1. Put ½ cup of water into a pan. Add 1 cup of sugar. Heat over low heat until sugar dissolves. Do not stir. Let it boil for one minute.
2. Pour the warm syrup into a glass or jar. Hang weighted string into the syrup. Let it stand at room temperature.
3. Large crystals will begin to form in about a week. You may need to break the crust to keep the water evaporating.

PIECES AND PATTERNS

# Nature's Part in Art...and Math

Identify, outline, and then draw the
major polygons in each picture.

Polygon means
a simple
closed
figure.

Tri = 3 ∴ a 3-sided polygon = a Triangle
Quad = 4 ∴ a 4-sided polygon = a Quadrilateral
Pent = 5 ∴ a 5-sided polygon = a Pentagon
Hex = 6 ∴ a 6-sided polygon = a Hexagon

"Hey - Have you
seen Wilbur?"

Spider Web

| Drawing | Name | Number of: | | |
| --- | --- | --- | --- | --- |
| | | Sides | Angles | Vertices |
| | | | | |
| | | | | |

Honey Comb

| Drawing | Name | Number of: | | |
| --- | --- | --- | --- | --- |
| | | Sides | Angles | Vertices |
| | | | | |
| | | | | |

PIECES AND PATTERNS

# Nature's Part in Art and Math

page #2

Name _____

Identify, outline and then draw the major polygons in each picture.

Citrus Fruit

| Drawing | Name | Number of: | | |
|---------|------|-------|--------|----------|
|         |      | Sides | Angles | Vertices |
|         |      |       |        |          |
|         |      |       |        |          |

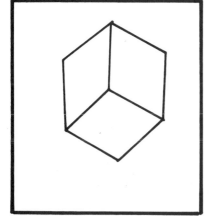

Sugar Crystal

| Drawing | Name | Number of: | | |
|---------|------|-------|--------|----------|
|         |      | Sides | Angles | Vertices |
|         |      |       |        |          |
|         |      |       |        |          |

Snowflake

| Drawing | Name | Number of: | | |
|---------|------|-------|--------|----------|
|         |      | Sides | Angles | Vertices |
|         |      |       |        |          |
|         |      |       |        |          |
|         |      |       |        |          |

42

© 1986 AIMS Education Foundation

PIECES AND PATTERNS

# Nature's Part in Art and Math

Name _____

| Drawing | Name | Number of: | | |
|---|---|---|---|---|
| | | Sides | Angles | Vertices |
| | | | | |
| | | | | |
| | | | | |

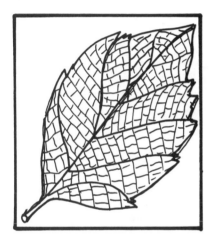

| Drawing | Name | Number of: | | |
|---|---|---|---|---|
| | | Sides | Angles | Vertices |
| | | | | |
| | | | | |

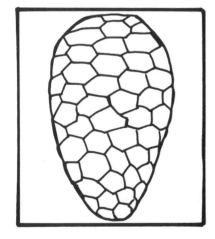

| Drawing | Name | Number of: | | |
|---|---|---|---|---|
| | | Sides | Angles | Vertices |
| | | | | |
| | | | | |

In a simple polygon, what is the relationship of sides, angles and vertices?

_____

43

# Triangles - Patchwork Patterns

45

**PIECES AND PATTERNS**

# Rhombii Patterns

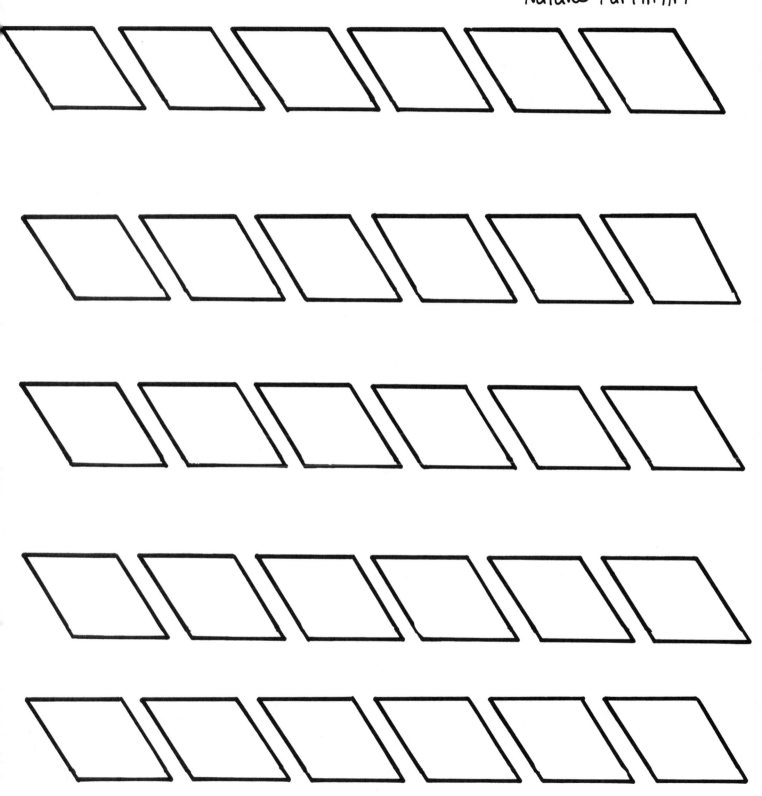

46

PIECES AND PATTERNS

# Trapezoids - Patchwork Patterns

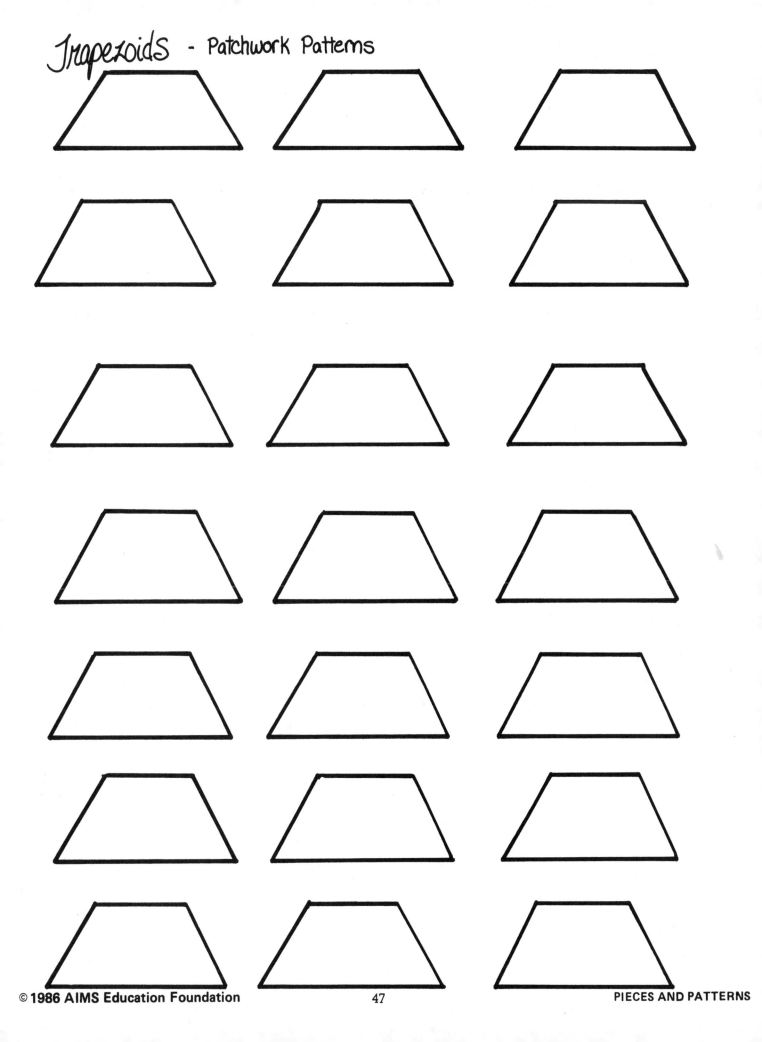

Hexagon Patterns for: Nature's Part in Art
Inside Job
Patchwork Patterns

48

PIECES AND PATTERNS

# An Inside Job

Will it tile?

## I. Topic Area
Symmetry and tessellating regular polygons.

## II. Introductory Statement
Students will explore the mathematics of why certain shapes "tile" and others do not.

## III. Math Skills
a. Geometry
b. Interior angles
c. Adding angles
d. Applying a formula
e. Equalities and inequalities

## Science Processes
a. Observing
b. Predicting
c. Analyzing data
d. Drawing conclutions

## IV. Materials
Regular polygon patterns in various colors
Scissors
Glue

## V. Key Question
Which regular polygons will tessellate and which will not? Why?

## VI. Educative Input
1. Regular polygons whose interior angle is a factor of 360 will tessellate. These are the equilateral triangle, square, and hexagon.
2. No regular polygon with more than 6 sides will tile the plane because the measure of an interior angle increases as the number of sides increases. The interior angle of a regular polygon must be less than 180 degrees. The interior angle of a regular polygon with 6 sides is 120 degrees.
3. Symmetry of non-living things often deals with the numbers 3, 4, or 6. Symmetry of living things often contains the number 5 commonly found in plants.
4. While a 5-sided regular polygon cannot tile a plane, we often find the pentagon in nature but they are not regular.

## VII. Management Suggestions
1. Even though the procedure is well defined, it would be wise to "walk through" the first two examples on the worksheet as a teacher directed experience. Then proceed independently.

## VIII. Procedure
1. Cut out regular polygon pattern pieces.
2. Count and record the number of sides of each.
3. On worksheet "An Inside Job..."
   a. Form triangles inside each polygon by drawing dotted line diagonals from the vertex marked with a star to each of the other vertices.
   b. Count the triangles formed and multiply by 180°.
   c. Divide by the number of sides in the regular polygon to get the number of degrees in each interior (inside) angle.
4. Use polygon patterns to tile around a single point. Make one complete revolution without gaps or overlaps. (You may trace the shape as you rotate it if you wish.)
5. Drawing conclusions: How can you tell which polygons tessellate?
6. Create Patchwork Patterns by tiling combinations of regular polygons from the patterns provided. Try:
   a. squares and triangles
   b. rhombi (diamonds) and trapezoids
   c. hexagons and free choice
   d. 2 or 3 polygons of free choice or try octagons and diamonds.

## IX. What the Students Will Do.
1. Explore the mathematical proof that illustrates why some regular polygons tessellate and others do not.
2. Create patterns by tiling combinations of regular polygons.

## X. Discussion
1. Do all regular polygons tessellate? (no)
2. What do you notice about the number of sides of a regular polygon and the size of the angle? (As you increase the number of sides, the size of the inside angle also increases.)

## XI. Extension
1. Try tessellating alphabet letters. Use upper case block letters. Try H. Some shapes of H will tile.

2. Create your own "tile". Begin with a regular shape like a square.
Whatever you do to one side, you must do likewise to the other.

PIECES AND PATTERNS

# An Inside Job

Cut out regular polygon patterns.
Place regular polygon pieces, side by side, clockwise around center point.
Record number of similar shapes that complete a cycle.

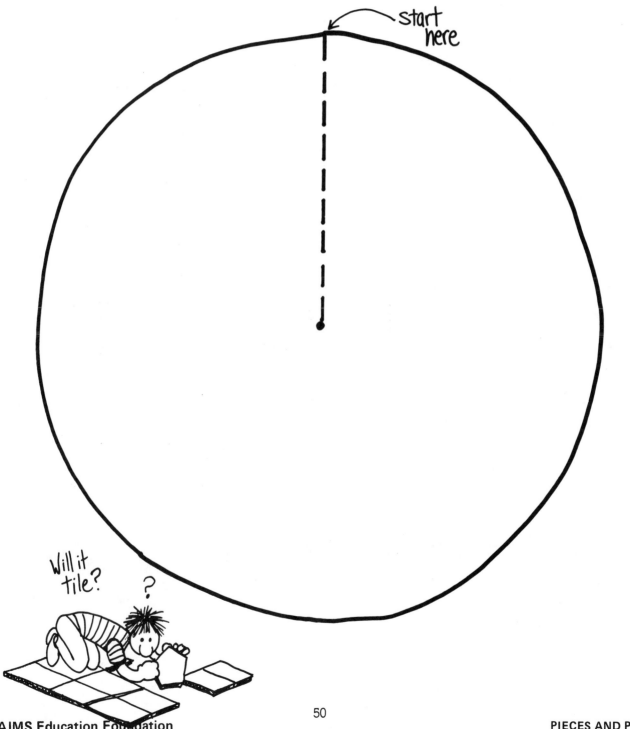

start here

Will it tile?

?

PIECES AND PATTERNS

# An Inside Job

To find the number of degrees in each inside angle of a regular polygon:
1. Form triangles inside each polygon by drawing diagonals from each ★. Count the triangles. Multiply by 180°.
2. Divide by number of sides in polygon.

| Regular Polygon | Number of Triangles ✗ 180° | | ÷ Number of Sides | = | Degrees in each inside angle of polygon |
|---|---|---|---|---|---|
| Equilateral Triangle | | | | | |
| Square | | | | | |
| Pentagon | | | | | |
| Hexagon | | | | | |
| Heptagon | | | | | |
| Octagon | | | | | |

PIECES AND PATTERNS

# An Inside Job

## Data Chart

| Regular Polygon | Predicted # of Polygons | Actual # of Polygons | # of degrees in inside Angle | Sum of Angles around center | Compare to 360° >< = | Will it tile Yes or No? |
|---|---|---|---|---|---|---|
| Triangle | | | | | | |
| Square | | | | | | |
| Pentagon | | | | | | |
| Hexagon | | | | | | |
| Heptagon | | | | | | |
| Octagon | | | | | | |

Drawing conclusions: (How can I tell which polygons will tile?)

All polygons that. . . . _____

The number of triangles formed is always 2 less than the number of sides in a regular polygon

52

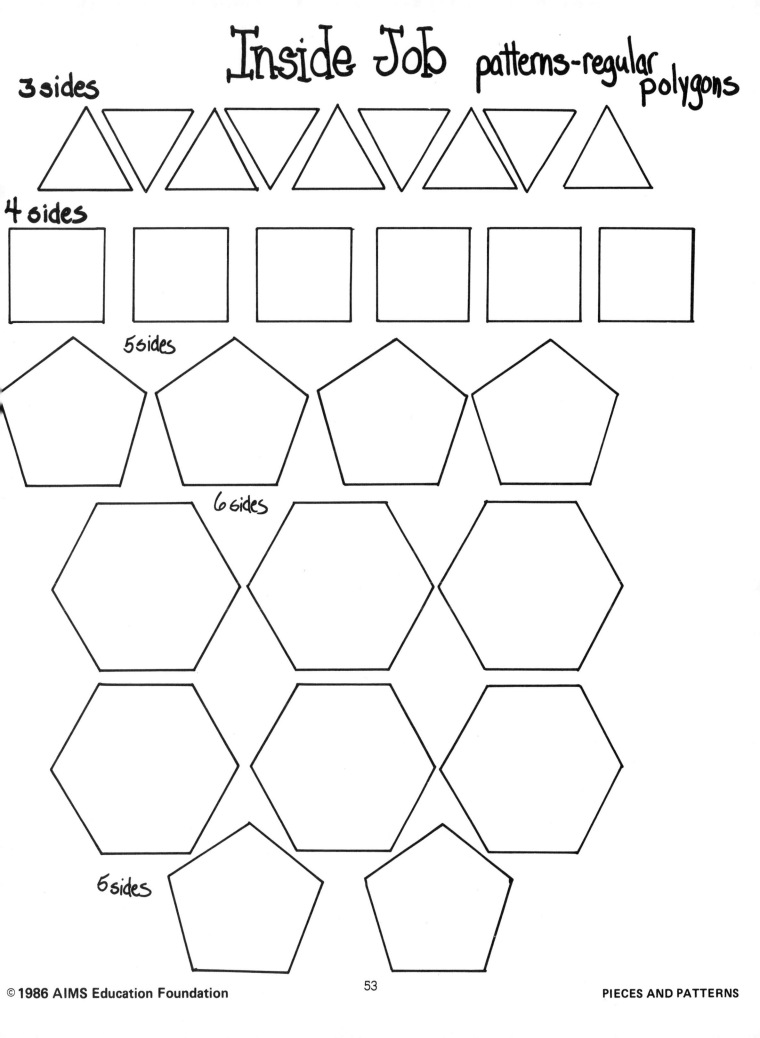

# Inside Job patterns-regular polygons

3 sides

4 sides

5 sides

6 sides

6 sides

**PIECES AND PATTERNS**

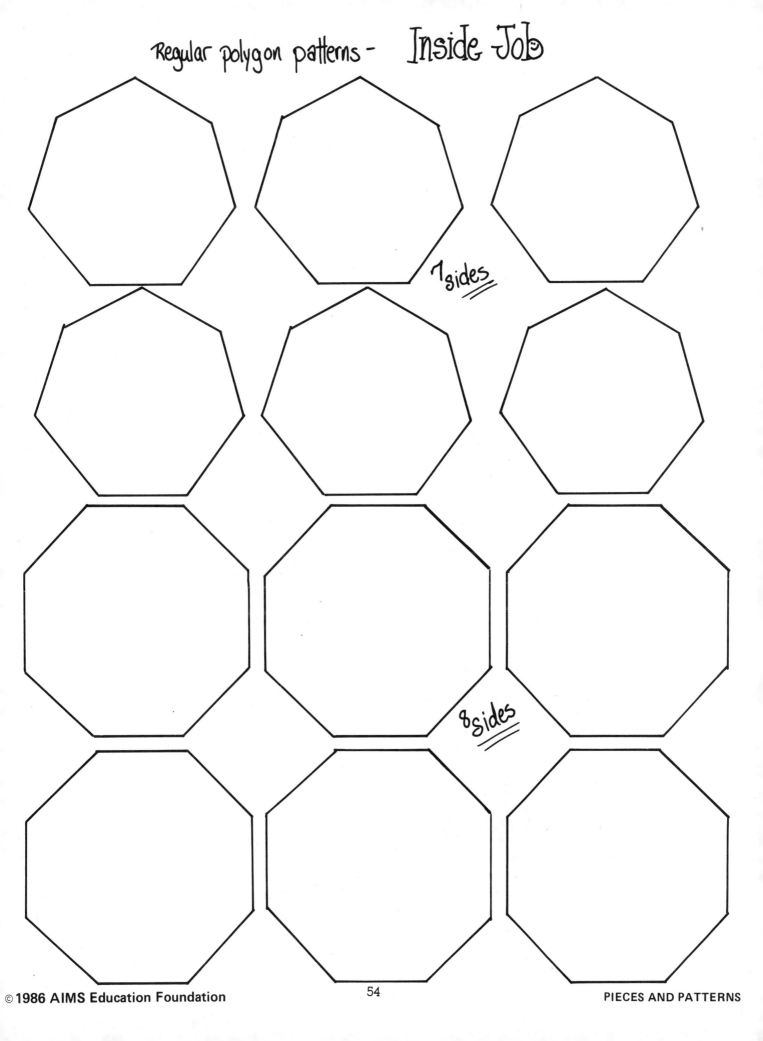

Regular polygon patterns - Inside Job

7 sides

8 sides

54

PIECES AND PATTERNS

# PATCHWORK PATTERNS

Which combinations of polygons will tessellate?

Try squares and triangles ☐ △

Try rhombi and trapezoids ▱ ▱

PIECES AND PATTERNS

# PATCHWORK PATTERNS

Try hexagons and_____ (your choice.)

Choose 2 or 3 polygons and tessellate:

PIECES AND PATTERNS

# ME AND MY SHADOW

## I. Topic Area
Shadows and their relationship to time of day.

## II. Introductory Statement
Students will measure the lengths of their shadows at different times of the day to determine when a shadow casts its longest and shortest image.

## III. Math Skills
a. Measuring
b. Problem solving
c. Logic
d. Comparing
e. Making a bar graph

## Science Processes
a. Observing
b. Predicting
c. Recording data
d. Interpreting
e. Generalizing

## IV. Materials
Meter tapes
Chalk
Butcher paper
Marking pens

## V. Key Question
At what time of day will my shadow appear the longest? the shortest?

## VI. Educative Input
1. Two factors are involved here: the height of the person casting the shadow, and the time of day the measurement is recorded.
2. Shadows are long when the light source (sun) is low (morning and late afternoon) and shorter when the sun is high (noon).

## VII. Management Suggestions
1. Students need to work in threes: one to cast the shadow, one to measure and one to record. Students may take turns at each job so that they have three sets of information.
2. You must choose a sunny day so that shadows will be vivid and easy to measure and trace.
3. Select 4 times during the day that are convenient for your students to measure shadows and that are well spaced over the day. Suggested times are 8:30, 10:30, 12:30, and 2:30.
4. Students need to position themselves on the same mark each time they measure their shadow.
5. Use chalk to draw around shadows on blacktop or use butcher paper and black markers to make paper tracings.

## VIII. Procedure
1. Have each student measure and record his own height.
2. Have students cast their shadows on blacktop or large sheets of paper and trace. Paper tracings could be brought indoors for display and comparison.
3. Measure and record length of shadow and time on the tracing.
4. Follow steps 2-3 at four time intervals during the day.
5. Compare the length of shadow cast at each time of day to your actual height.
6. Discuss how the length of a shadow changes during the day.

## IX. What the Students Will Do
1. Measure and record their own height in metric units.
2. Measure and record lengths of their shadows at four pre-determined times during the day.
3. Organize and display data into a graph.
4. Generalize information regarding the conditions that determine the lengthening or shortening of their shadows.
5. Compare their actual height to the length of their shadows at selected times.

## X. Discussion
1. What is a shadow? (A shadow is a dark image formed when an object obstructs the path of light.)
2. How does the size of the shadow cast compare to the size of the actual object?
3. At what time of day will I have the longest possible shadow? (early morning or late afternoon)
4. How did the shadows change during the day?
5. What causes the shadows to move?
6. Was there a pattern in the shadow's movement?
7. Could a shadow's movement be predicted?

## XI. Extensions
1. Trace the shadow of an object like a tall bottle onto a large piece of newsprint at hourly intervals during the day. Discuss the movement of the shadows.
2. Do a comparison study of shadows during another season of the year.
3. Figure the surface area of the shadows cast at various times during the day. Use centimeter grid paper to record.
4. See *Sun Watchers* to make sun dial watches.

**PIECES AND PATTERNS**

NAME _____

# ME AND MY SHADOW

Predictions:
What time of day will your shadow be:
the longest? _____
the shortest? _____

Is my shadow longer or shorter than my actual height at these times:

ME                                    my shadow

| CENTIMETERS | | | | | | | | | |
|---|---|---|---|---|---|---|---|---|---|
| 275 | | | | | | | | | |
| 250 | | | | | | | | | |
| 225 | | | | | | | | | |
| 200 | | | | | | | | | |
| 175 | | | | | | | | | |
| 150 | | | | | | | | | |
| 125 | | | | | | | | | |
| 100 | | | | | | | | | |
| 75 | | | | | | | | | |
| 50 | | | | | | | | | |
| 25 | | | | | | | | | |
| 0 | | | | | | | | | |

— — — — — — — — —
Times

58

PIECES AND PATTERNS

# SunWatchers

## I. Topic Area
Shadows and sundials

## II. Introductory Statement
Students will use the angle of the shadows cast by a meter stick to learn about the time of day and then apply that information to construct a sundial watch.

## III. Math Skills
a. Measuring angles
b. Recording time
c. Using a protractor
d. Fractions

## Science Processes
a. Observing
b. Recording data
c. Interpreting data
d. Generalizing information

## IV. Materials
Meter stick or doweling rod
Protractor for each student
Large protractor for teacher demonstration
Sun dial watch pattern for each student
Card stock (index cards)
Spool of sturdy thread or fine polished twine
Needle with large eye
Scissors
Glue

## V. Key Question
How can we use shadows to tell the time of day?

## VI. Educative Input
1. Sundials and clocks both indicate time but don't always agree on what time of day it is. Clocks are based on days of equal length. A sundial measures solar time and will not be satisfactory for precise time keeping. Also a sun dial divides daylight into 12 hours. But all days do not have equal hours of daylight—summer days are longer than winter.
2. To construct an accurate sun dial, it is necessary to adjust it to the latitude where it will be used. In this activity, the pattern shown is constructed for approximately 40 degrees North latitude.
3. Distance from the fold line to point B (horizontal) is 6 cm and the distance from fold line to point A (vertical) is 5 cm. The two faces must be at right angles when opened and the angle of the string with the horizontal face will measure 45 degrees.

## VII. Management Suggestions
1. Plan to do this activity on two consecutive sunny days.
2. On Day 1: Use a large protractor to demonstrate the correct way of measuring angles. Measure the angle of each shadow cast at hourly intervals. Point out that two angles are formed with the base line and that it is more efficient to measure the lesser of the two.
3. On Day 2: Test results and compare to previous day's data. Culminate activity by constructing sun dial watches.

## VIII. Procedure
1. *Day 1:* Find a location on the school yard where the blacktop runs east and west and edges a grassy area on the south. Insert a meter stick or doweling rod into the ground between the grass and the blacktop. See diagram.
2. Using a large protractor, demonstrate how to measure the angle of the stick's shadow to the base line formed by the blacktop against the grass area. Measure the most efficient angle.
3. Measure these shadow angles hourly and record.
4. Return to the classroom and have students use the angle measurements recorded to construct a paper model of a sun dial. Measure and mark each angle and connect it to the base line. Mark each angle with the appropriate time.
5. *Day 2:* Test the results of the paper model sun dial by returning to the playground at times that match Day 1. Insert a pencil in the place on the worksheet marked to draw in shadow lines cast at each time interval.
6. Construct a sun dial watch following instructions on pattern provided.
7. Use sun dial watch at random times during the day to record solar time to the nearest quarter hour. Compare to actual time.

## IX. What the Students Will Do
1. Observe how to use protractor to measure angles of shadows cast on blacktop. Record angle and time.
2. Use a protractor to construct angles of shadows and test measurements on a paper model of a sun dial.
3. Construct a sun dial watch and record solar time to the nearest quarter hour. Compare to actual time.

## X. Discussion
1. How are solar time and actual time (clock time) different?
2. How does a shadow give us information about the time of day?

## XI. Extension
1. Discuss an "Anywhere Sundial"

Place a reasonably straight stick or pencil between your thumb and index finger. Hold your palm out flat so the stick makes a shadow. In the morning, use your left hand and point your fingers west. In the afternoon use your right hand and point your fingers east. Angle the stick towards the north so that the shadow is long enough to fill the whole hand.

PIECES AND PATTERNS

# SunWatchers

## DAY #1:

*Use a protractor to measure the angle of each shadow cast by these time intervals. Record your data here:

| Time | 9:00am | 10:00am | 11:00am | 12:00am | 1:00am | 2:00am | 3:00am |
|------|--------|---------|---------|---------|--------|--------|--------|
| Angle | ° ___ | ° ___ | ° ___ | ° ___ | ° ___ | ° ___ | ° ___ |

* Use these angle measurements to construct a paper model of a sundial that will show time:

1. Measure and mark each angle, then connect it to the baseline.
2. Record the appropriate time for each reading.

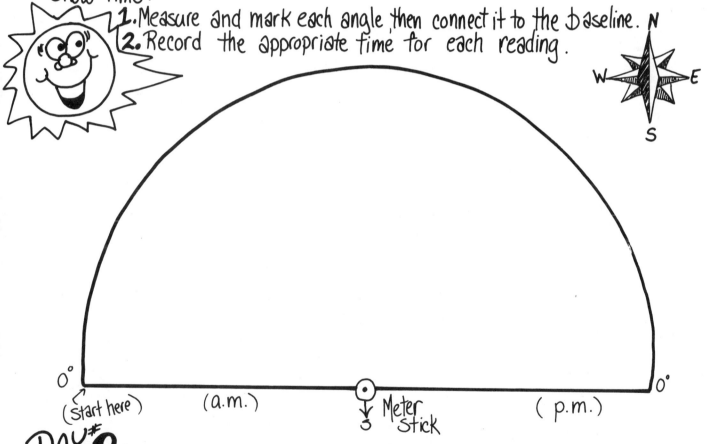

0° (start here)   (a.m.)   ↓S Meter Stick   (p.m.)   0°

## DAY #2:

Test your results: Return to the play ground. Insert a pencil in the place marked meter stick. Face the south and use a colored pencil to draw in the shadow line cast at each time interval.

How closely do they match yesterday's recordings? Explain: _____

# SunWatchers

## Directions

1. Cut out sundial watch.
2. Reinforce pattern by gluing it to a larger piece of cardboard or tagboard.
3. Cut away excess cardboard
4. Fold on dotted fold line
5. Fasten sturdy string from point A to point B so that when the watch is open, it forms a right (90°) angle.

6. Anchor ends of string with tape.
7. Decorate outside cover (optional)
8. The arrow must be pointing South ( ŝ ) when using the watch.
9. A hole may be punched in tab above point A. Insert long string and hang around your neck.

Use your new watch at random times during the day. Record solar to the nearest quarter hour.

How accurate am I? _____

| | A | B | C | D | E |
|---|---|---|---|---|---|
| Solar Time | | | | | |
| Actual Time | | | | | |
| Difference | | | | | |

61

© 1986 AIMS Education Foundation

PIECES AND PATTERNS

 Water Activities

## I. Topic Area

Water and surface tension

## II. Introductory Statement

Through a series of water activities, students will explore the properties of water and the phenomenon of surface tension.

## III. Math Skills

a. Counting
b. Estimating
c. Graphing
d. Problem solving
e. Surface area
f. Volume

## Science Processes

a. Observing
b. Collecting data
c. Hypothesizing
d. Predicting
e. Applying and generalizing

## IV. Materials

5 clear round containers of various sizes
Eye droppers
Pennies
Nickels
Paper towels
Water source

## VI. Key Question

Which of the lettered containers, A-E, when filled to the rim with water, will hold the greatest number of pennies before the water spills over?

## VI. Educative Input

1. The tendency of water to act as if it has a very thin membrane stretched over it is called surface tension. It has many effects. It is responsible for the phenomenon of water tending to form drops rather than spreading out into some other shape. It also is responsible for the "dome" shape that results when you pile drops of water on a penny.

2. Questions concerning surface tension might be addressed in this manner:

   Water molecules have an attraction for each other. These molecules are equally attracted in every direction in the center of the cup of water. On the top or surface of the water they are attracted only by the water molecules next to each other or beneath them. On the sides next to the container, these water molecules are pulled down or to the center. They are simply like water molecules holding hands; thus creating a dome-like shape. Regarding a molecule: it is simply a matter of size. The whole is made up of parts some so small we cannot see them.

3. The choice of 5 containers should purposely include a range in volume from small to tall, but in order to build the idea of surface tension and provide a discrepant event, make sure the largest container (in volume) has a narrow or small mouth. Many students are sure that the largest container will hold the greatest number of pennies when, in fact, the number of pennies held before the water spills over is directly related to the size of the exposed surface area of the mouth of the glass or jar.

   Suggested containers include: plastic medicine cup, small plastic drinking cup, small baby food jar, tall apple juice jar with narrow mouth.

4. In a discussion of the properties of water and the phenomenon of surface tension, compile all the contributions of the students on the overhead or large piece of butcher paper. The verbal exchange of ideas is an excellent way to share different ways of expressing similar ideas.

## VII. Management Suggestions

1. This activity should be a directed total class experience but youngsters may work cooperatively in groups of 2, 3, or 4.
2. Provide plenty of paper towels for spillage.
3. You may wish to discuss acceptable behavior when doing water activities.
4. It might be wise to remind students to exercise caution trying not to jar the table or desk where students are working. Some students may wish to use the floor as the most level surface available.
5. Take advantage of sharing group observations so that students may "teach" one another.

## VIII. Procedure

1. Display 5 containers, arranged from small to tall and labeled A-E. Predict which container, when filled to the rim with water, will hold the greatest number of pennies.
2. Sketch the shape of each container.
3. Distribute a small glass of water to each group of students. Observe and describe the water in terms of its properties. Use your senses—sight, smell, sound, feel, and taste.
4. Share the observations as a class. Use descriptions that you understand and can explain to others.
5. Estimate the number of drops of water than can be piled on a penny before it spills over. Record.

6. Distribute eye droppers and paper towels. Count drops and record on "eye dropper" graphs.

7. Observe and describe what you "see" as the water "piles up" on the penny. Record and prepare to discuss observations.

8. Try same activity with another coin: a nickel or other side of the penny.

9. Share observations regarding the "pile of water".

10. Share and discuss data collected.

11. Refer to original containers A-E. Assign one container to each group and perform "penny drop". Drop pennies into full cup of water. Count and record.

12. Share data. Compare and discuss the likenesses and differences of containers.

13. Write a generalization that explains why any given container holds more than another. (widest mouth has greatest surface area.)

## IX. What the Students Will Do

1. Predict which of 5 containers when filled with water, will hold the most pennies.

2. Observe and describe the properties of a glass of water.

3. Estimate the number of drops of water than can be piled on a penny.

4. Count and record drops of water that can be piled on a penny, a nickel.

5. Observe and describe phenomenon of "surface tension".

6. Count and record number of pennies that can be dropped into containers filled with water.

7 Compare data.

8. Write a generalization that explains data collected.

## X. Discussion

1. Do all of the containers, when filled with water, hold the same number of pennies before spilling over? (no)

2. What are some of your observations about the properties of water? (Typical comments may include: It's clear. It makes things look bigger. It moves. It makes pencil look bent in it. It feels cool.)

3. How many drops can be piled on a penny? (a wide range).

4. What variables are responsible for that range in number? (age of penny, side of penny, composition of penny, size of water drop.)

5. What does "surface tension" look like? (curved like a lens, jello-like, stretched like a net holding it together).

6. Which container, when filled with water, holds the most pennies before "spill-over"?

7. How is that container different from the others?

## XI. Extensions

1. Encourage further exploration by posing these questions:
   a. Does the temperature of the water make a difference? Try ice water and hot water. Compare results.
   b. Do other liquids behave in a like manner? Try rubbing alcohol or cooking oil.
   c. What happens when you add liquid soap or salt?

2. Given two water filled containers, one with an exposed surface area twice as large as the other, will it hold twice the number of pennies? Try it.

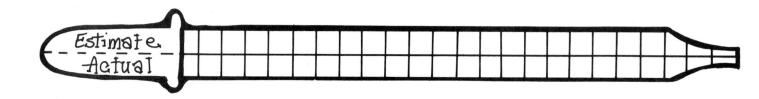

63

# Water Activities

**1.** Predict which one of 5 containers, A-E, when filled with water holds the greatest number of pennies before it spills over.

My Prediction _____        Actual _____

Please sketch the shape of each container:

|  |  |  |  |  |
|---|---|---|---|---|
| A | B | C | D | E |

**2.** Observe a glass of water and describe what you see. Tell me all you can about water.... using your senses:

1. _____
2. _____
3. _____
4. _____
5. _____

**3.** Estimate the number of drops of water that you think can be "piled" on a penny before it spills over.

Estimate _____        Actual _____

Record on the "eye dropper" graph.

PENNY

| Estimate |
| Actual |

Number of drops of water

64          PIECES AND PATTERNS

# Water Activities (cont.)

Write 5 words or phrases that describe what you see or observe as the water "piles" on a penny.

1._____
2._____
3._____
4._____
5._____

How about a nickel? More drops or less?? Circle one. Explain why.

## Nickel

| Estimate | | | | | | | | | | | | | | | | |
|----------|---|---|---|---|---|---|---|---|---|---|---|---|---|---|---|---|
| Actual | | | | | | | | | | | | | | | | |

Number of drops of water

4.) Compare data. Are all the results the same? Why? What factors influence the number of drops on a coin?

5.) Do you wish to change your prediction regarding which container will hold the greatest number of pennies?

## Data Table

| Container | Number of Pennies |
|-----------|-------------------|
| A | |
| B | |
| C | |
| D | |
| E | |

Write a generalization that explains the data collected in this table.

_____
_____
_____
_____

1. What happens when you add liquid soap?
2. Does the temperature of water make a difference?
3. Try other liquids.

# A Nutty Experience

## I. Topic Area
Heat energy and calories.

## II. Introductory Statement
Students will compare the heat energy released in burning several kinds of nuts.

## III. Math Skills
a. Measuring
b. Temperature
c. Logic
d. Applying a formula

## Science Processes
a. Estimating
b. Predicting
c. Controlling variables
d. Recording data
e. Appllying and generalizing

## IV. Materials
Assorted fresh nuts, shelled
Paper clips (small)
Small glass beaker (5)
Tuna or soup can (5)
Matches
Thermometers (5)
Balance scale
Masses

## V. Key Question
Which has more heat energy (calories): a peanut or a walnut?

## VI. Educative Input
1. Energy is measured by calculating the amount of heat produced when food is burned.
2. Define calorie: The amount of heat energy needed to raise the temperature of 1 gram (1 ml) of water one degree centigrade is one calorie. This is not to be confused with the "calorie" referred to in nutrition which is really a kilocalorie. One $kcal = 10^3$ cal.

## VII. Management Suggestions
1. For the sake of safety, this activity must be well monitored.

## VIII. Procedure
1. Weigh equal amounts of nut meat.
2. Bend a paper clip as a stand for the nut. See illustration:
3. Measure 100 ml of water into each glass beaker.
4. Place paper clip stand with nut meat under the vented tuna or soup can.
5. Place beaker with water on top of tuna can. Place thermometer in water.
6. Record water temperature at start $(T_1)$.
7. Set fire to the nut meat and record temperature of water $(T_2)$ when nut meat is completely burned up.
8. Record the difference in temperatures from start to finish $(T_1 - T_2)$.
9. Compute the number of calories by using the formula: Calories = ml of water × change in temp. or $C = $ ml of water × $(T_1 - T_2)$.
10. Record data on worksheet.
11. Use centimeter graph paper and construct a bar graph that displays the number of calories burned for each kind of nut meat. Be sure to title the graph and label both axes.

## IX. What the Students Will Do
1. Shell and then weigh equal amounts of various kinds of nut meats.
2. Measure water and record temperature.
3. Ignite nut meats. Measure and record resulting temperature change of water.
4. Record caloric amount for each nut.
5. Compare results among various nut meats.
6. Construct a bar graph that displays results.

## X. Discussion Questions
1. Do all nut meats of equal amounts produce the same amount of heat?
2. Which nuts have the most calories? the least? the same?
3. Some nut meats ignite and burn more rapidly than others. From your observations, what seems to cause this? (Some nut meats seem to have more natural oil than others.)

## XI. Extensions
1. Compare calories burned in an equal amount of other foods such as: marshmallow, piece of hot dog, or a potato chip.
2. Make peanut butter from each of the varieties...by processing in a blender. How many nuts does it take to produce a cup of "peanut" or "almond" butter?
3. Do a cost analysis of peanut butter and almond butter.

PIECES AND PATTERNS

# A NUTTY EXPERIENCE

1. Weigh equal amounts of nut meat.
2. Measure 100ml of water into a glass beaker. Record starting temperature (T₁).
3. Place paper clip stand with nut meat under tin can. Ignite nut meat.
4. Place beaker of water on top of tin can. Insert thermometer in water.
5. Record water temperature when nut meat is completely burned up (T₂).
6. Figure change in water temperature (T₂-T₁). Record.
7. To determine calories: multiply amount of water times change in temperature. Record.
8. Record.

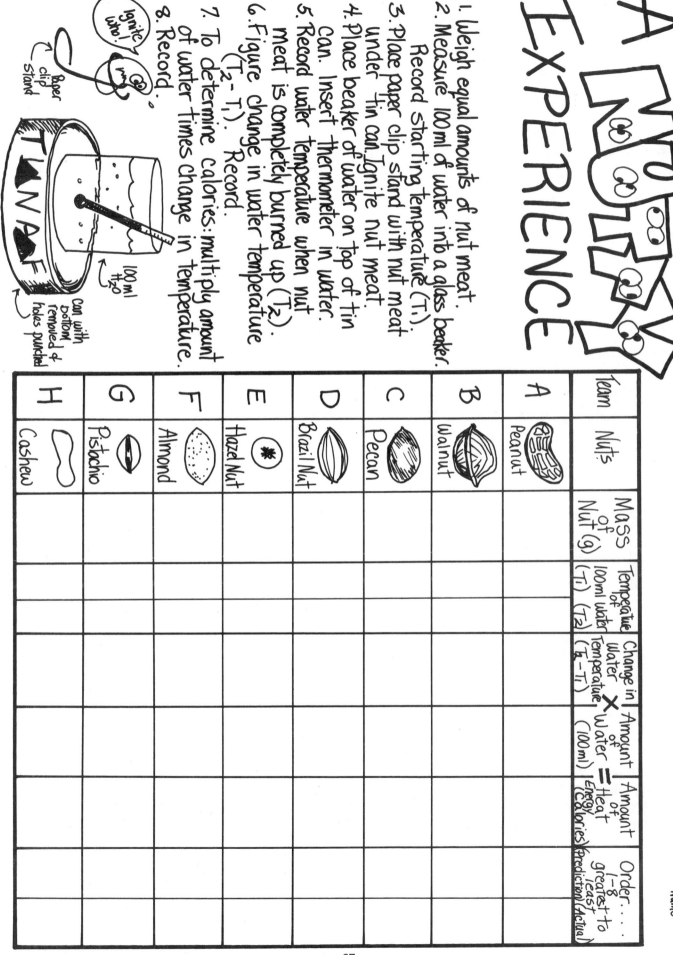

| Team | Nuts | Mass of Nut (g) | Temperature of 100ml water (T₁) | Water Temperature (T₂) | Change in Water Temperature (T₂-T₁) | Amount of Water (100ml) X Temperature = Amount of Heat Energy (Calories) | Order.... 1-8 greatest to least (Prediction/Actual) |
|---|---|---|---|---|---|---|---|
| A | Peanut | | | | | | |
| B | Walnut | | | | | | |
| C | Pecan | | | | | | |
| D | Brazil Nut | | | | | | |
| E | Hazel Nut | | | | | | |
| F | Almond | | | | | | |
| G | Pistachio | | | | | | |
| H | Cashew | | | | | | |

Name _____

PIECES AND PATTERNS

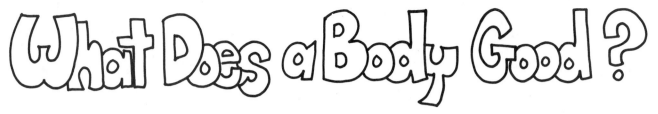

# What Does a Body Good ?

### I. Topic Area
Nutrients and Recommended Daily Allowances

### II. Introductory Statement
Students will become better acquainted with essential nutrients in various foods and better able to classify foods by their nutrient strengths.

### III. Math Skills
a. Percent
b. Graphing
c. Whole number computation
d. Constructing a table
e. Problem solving

### Science Processes
a. Observing
b. Classifying
c. Recording data
d. Applying and generalizing

### IV. Materials
Nutrition labels from various foods
Crayons or colored pens or pencils

### V. Key Question
Which has more nutrient value: a piece of cheese pizza or a Big Mac type hamburger?

### VI. Educative Input
1. In its widest sense, nutrition has to do with nourishing or supplying the ingredients necessary for the maintenance of life.
2. Most foods have some caloric value but many "junk" foods are high in calories and low in nutrient value.
3. Define R.D.A. (Recommended Daily Allowance). R.D.A. refers to the amounts of essential nutrients considered to be adequate to meet known nutritional needs of healthy people as derived by the Food and Drug Administration.
4. Nutrients are chemical substances obtained from food during digestion. *Essential* nutrients are those that the body cannot make or is unable to make in sufficient amounts to nourish itself. All of the 50 or so nutrients known to be needed by people can be classified into six categories: protein, carbohydrates, fat, vitamins, minerals, and water.
5. Nutrient information listed on foods is voluntary unless a manufacturer adds nutrients or makes a nutritional claim on a label or in advertising. It is then mandatory.

### VII. Management
1. If possible, start a collection of a variety of food labels containing nutrient information well ahead of scheduled activity. This will provide a "bank" of food labels from which to choose. Students may also copy information from labels at home or store.
2. Save complete label from food so that additional information such as cost and advertising claims may be further analyzed.

3. Students may wish to consult a Calorie Counter for parts of the activity. Calorie charts may be found in many cookbooks or encyclopedias.

### VIII. Procedure
1. Collect food labels containing nutrient information.
2. Record information on labels provided on student worksheets.
3. Graph the nutrients. Color in each bar as indicated to show percentage of R.D.A.
4. Sort and classify foods according to nutrients.
5. Using a calorie guide, plan a nutritionally balanced day. Students must use all 2400 calories and show appropriate number of servings in each of the food groups.
6. Organize information into a Table and construct a circle graph to show Food Group proportions to total 2400 calorie allotment.

### IX. What the Students Will Do
1. Collect food labels containing nutrient information.
2. Record and analyze nutritional information.
3. Graph the nutritional information.
4. Sort and classify foods according to eight essential nutrients.
5. Plan a 2400 calorie nutritionally balanced day and display in a circle graph.

### X. Discussion Questions
1. Which foods provide large percentages of each nutrient?
2. Which foods are high in more than half the nutrients?
3. Are any foods high in all the nutrients?
4. Which foods have "empty" calories? That is, show relatively no or very low quantities of nutrients?

### XI. Extensions
1. Identify the major vitamins and their respective functions and sources.
2. Choose a fruit or vegetable and research its origin and uses. Organize and write a Fruit and Vegetable Trivia Game by having students submit questions and answers from their research.
3. Write to the Food and Drug Administration, Washington, D.C. 20204 for answers to questions on ingredients and nutrition information of various foods.
4. See: "Good for Me! (All About Food in 32 Bites)" by Marilyn Burns (Little, Brown & Co.). This is an excellent resource of creative ideas to enhance the study of food and nutrition.

# What Does a Body Good?

BC B₁ B₂ A

Find 2 foods at home with nutritional information.
Record that information on the labels provided here:

**#1 Food name and Brand** _____

Serving size _____
**Nutritional Information (per serving):**   Servings per container _____

Calories _____   Protein _____   Carbohydrate _____   Fat _____

**Percentage of U.S. recommended Daily Allowance (U.S.R.D.A.):**

Protein _____
Vitamin A _____
Vitamin C _____
Thiamin (B₁) _____

Riboflavin (B₂) _____
Niacin _____
Calcium _____
Iron _____

**#2 Food name and Brand** _____

Serving size _____
**Nutritional Information (per serving):**   Servings per container _____

Calories _____   Protein _____   Carbohydrate _____   Fat _____

**Percentage of U.S. recommended Daily Allowance (U.S.R.D.A.):**

Protein _____
Vitamin A _____
Vitamin C _____
Thiamine (B₁) _____

Riboflavin (B₂) _____
Niacin _____
Calcium _____
Iron _____

69

PIECES AND PATTERNS

# What Does a Body Good?

Name _____

Graph the nutrients.
Color in each bar as labeled.

Serving size _____
Calories _____

% of R.D.A.

Name of Food and Brand

| 100% | | | | | | | | |
|---|---|---|---|---|---|---|---|---|
| 96 | | | | | | | | |
| 92 | | | | | | | | |
| 88 | | | | | | | | |
| 84 | | | | | | | | |
| 80 | | | | | | | | |
| 76 | | | | | | | | |
| 72 | | | | | | | | |
| 68 | | | | | | | | |
| 64 | | | | | | | | |
| 60 | | | | | | | | |
| 56 | | | | | | | | |
| 52 | | | | | | | | |
| 48 | | | | | | | | |
| 44 | | | | | | | | |
| 40 | | | | | | | | |
| 36 | | | | | | | | |
| 32 | | | | | | | | |
| 28 | | | | | | | | |
| 24 | | | | | | | | |
| 20 | | | | | | | | |
| 16 | | | | | | | | |
| 12 | | | | | | | | |
| 8 | | | | | | | | |
| 4 | | | | | | | | |
| 0 | Protein Red | Vitamin A Yellow | Vitamin C Orange | Thiamin ($B_1$) Blue | Riboflavin ($B_2$) Green | Niacin Brown | Calcium Pink | Iron Purple |

PIECES AND PATTERNS

# What Does a Body Good?

## · One Day · Planning Sheet ·

### Plan a balanced diet that totals 2400 calories

| Food Group | # of Servings | Food Choices | # of Calories |
|---|---|---|---|
| Dairy Products | 4 | _____ | _____ |
| | | _____ | _____ |
| | | _____ | _____ |
| | | total | _____ |
| Meat & Fish | 2 | _____ | _____ |
| | | _____ | _____ |
| | | total | _____ |
| Fruit & Vegetable | 4 | _____ | _____ |
| | | _____ | _____ |
| | | _____ | _____ |
| | | _____ | _____ |
| | | total | _____ |
| Grain , Cereal | 4 | _____ | _____ |
| | | _____ | _____ |
| | | _____ | _____ |
| | | _____ | _____ |
| | | total | _____ |
| Other | | _____ | _____ |
| | | total | _____ |

PIECES AND PATTERNS

# What Does a Body Good?

- Let the circle represent the recommended daily allotment for boys and girls (7-14 years old) - 2400 calories.

- Use the totals from your planning sheet and divide the circle below into 5 sections, Milk & Dairy Products, Meat & Fish, Fruit & Vegetable, Grain & Cereals, and Other.

- Each section should represent the correct percentage of the total 2400 calories.

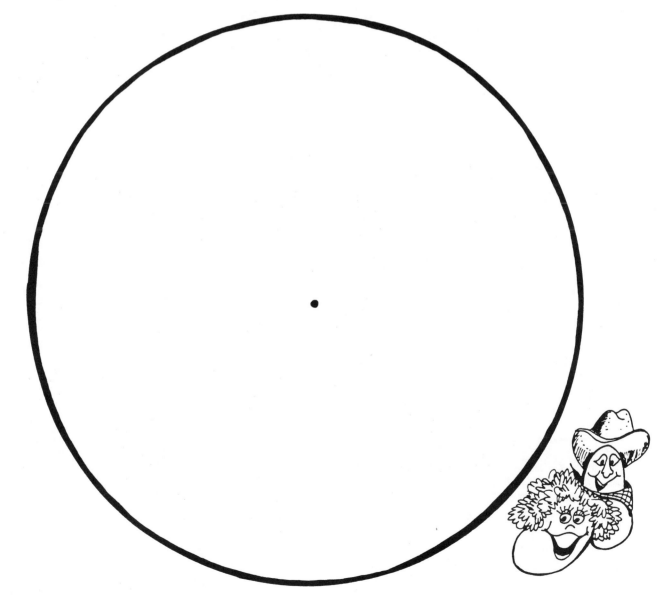

72

PIECES AND PATTERNS

# Practically Predictable

## I. Topic Area
The scientific method and statistics.

## II. Introductory Statement
Students will form and test a prediction and graph the results using the scientific method.

## III. Math Skills
a. Graphing
b. Logic
c. Making a table
d. Fractions
e. Percents
f. Ratios

## Science Processes
a. Forming a hypothesis
b. Collecing data
c. Interpreting data
d. Predicting
e. Generalizing information

## IV. Materials
Colored pencils

## V. Key Question
Can you make a prediction and prove it?

## VI. Educative Input
1. Prepare students for formulating a prediction by brainstorming a wide variety of ideas from which to choose a "question" to be explored. Build confidence by listing many ideas on chalkboard. (See suggested questions from which to begin.)
2. Guide students in selecting a question that will give a specific and predictable number of responses. This will insure more success in graphing the results.
3. From the questions to be asked, discuss appropriate terminology for making a prediction or hypothesis. For example:

    I predict that 50% of the people surveyed will or will not...

    I predict that 8 out of 15 of the people surveyed will or will not...

    I predict ¾ of the people surveyed will or will not...

    I predict that all or none will...
4. Discuss appropriate places to collect data... grocery store, school, classroom, church... places that are known to you and your family and that are safe.
5. You may wish to discuss sampling techniques and the large numbers necessary to confirm a prediction or hypothesis.

## VII. Management Suggestions
1. Use "I Scream for Ice Cream" as a teacher directed structured example. Follow described procedure. Use "open" worksheet as a follow up on their own.
2. Students may wish to work in pairs or teams to select a prediction and collect data together.
3. Some prior graphing experience is highly recommended because students will be diagnosing and constructing their own graphs.

## VIII. Procedure
1. Select a topic of general interest such as ice cream flavors.
2. With a partner formulate a question to be asked of all participants.
3. Determine number of people to be surveyed and make a prediction. Use one of the three suggested formats on the student worksheet. Record prediction on a separate piece of paper and turn in to teacher.
4. Collect data. Keep a tally of responses and organize into a table.
5. Construct a graph that best displays the data collected.
6. Compare your predictions with your results.
7. Write two true statements that generalize the data collected.
8. Share conclusions with class.

## IX. What the Students Will Do
1. Write a hypothesis or a prediction.
2. Collect data and keep a tally.
3. Organize data into a table.
4. Design and construct a graph to share results.
5. Analyze and generalize data to prove or disprove a prediction or hypthesis.

## X. Discussion
1. Evaluate kinds of questions that are optimal for a survey. (specific and predictable answers).
2. How are surveys a good or bad sampling technique in making predictions?
3. Explain this idea: "You don't have to eat the whole ox to know the meat is tough."

## XI. Extension
1. Apply "scientific method" to the selection of a science project for the science fair.

73

# Sample I. I scream for Ice Cream

1. Topic: Ice cream flavors

2. Question: Of these 7 flavors, which ice cream is your favorite? (list 7 flavors)
   ① _____  ② _____  ③ _____  ④ _____  ⑤ _____
   ⑥ _____  ⑦ _____

3. Prediction: I predict that:
   ⓐ _____ % of the people surveyed will like _____ best.
   ⓑ _____ out of _____ people will like _____ flavor best.
   or ⓒ ___/___ (fraction) of the people surveyed prefer _____ ice cream.

4. Tally: Keep a tally of the responses and organize into a table.

| Flavors | (1) | (2) | (3) | (4) | (5) | (6) | (7) |
|---|---|---|---|---|---|---|---|
| # of persons Tally | | | | | | | |
| Total Number | | | | | | | |

5. Construct a graph that best displays the data collected:

Number of Persons (y-axis: 7, 6, 5, 4, 3, 2, 1)

Flavors (x-axis: 1, 2, 3, 4, 5, 6, 7)

6. Conclusion:
   My prediction proved to be true or untrue (circle one)

7. Write 2 true statements that sum up the data collected.
   ⓐ _____
   ⓑ _____

© 1986 AIMS Education Foundation

PIECES AND PATTERNS

# Practically Predictable

1. Topic: _____

2. Question: _____
_____

3. Prediction: (be sure to express your prediction as a per cent, a fraction, or a ratio)
   I predict that _____
   _____

4. Tally: Keep a tally of responses for each person surveyed. Organize the data collected into a table.

5. Construct a graph that best displays the data collected. (ie: bar, line, or circle graph).

6. Conclusion: My prediction proved to be true or untrue. (circle one)

7. Write a true statement about the data collected.
_____
_____
_____

75

**PIECES AND PATTERNS**

# Practically Predictable
## 20 Questions to Choose From

1. How tall are you?

2. What's your favorite music group?

3. How often do you brush your teeth?

4. How many desserts do you eat per week?

5. What's your favorite color? (animal, candy bar, cereal, show etc.)

6. How many hours per week do you spend watching T.V.?

7. How well can you spell (given 10 words)

8. What are you most afraid of?

9. How many hours sleep do you get each night?

10. Of the numbers 1, 2, 3, or 4, which one would you choose?

11. Which soft drink do you drink most often?

12. How do you prefer to spend your leisure time?

13. What kind of pet do you own?

14. How many T.V.'s do you have in your home?

15. How many hours a week do you exercise?

16. Can you name the 7 continents and 4 oceans?

17. Are you a native Californian? In what state were you born?

18. What nervous habit do you have? What do you do when you are nervous?

19. Are you right or left handed?

20. How do you rate yourself on a scale of 1-10?

76

PIECES AND PATTERNS

# Turtle Trips and Turns

## I. Topic Area
Turtle graphics and geometry.

## II. Introductory Statement
Students are introduced to "turtle graphics" and hands-on experiences to acquaint them with LOGO language and behavior and related problem solving strategies.

## III. Math Skills
a. Geometry
b. Measuring angles
c. Spatial relationships
d. Logic
e. Applying a formula

### Science Processes
a. Observing
b. Predicting
c. Recording data
d. Controlling variables
e. Applying and generalizing

## IV. Materials
Clear Thermofax transparencies
   7 for reproducing protractors (4 per page = 28)
   4 for reproducing turtles (9 per page = 36)
Sewing snaps—size 4/0, one per turtle
Scissors
Large needle or compass point for piercing a hole

## V. Key Question
How can I command a turtle to draw a picture?

## VI. Educative Input
1. By "playing turtle", students act out simple LOGO commands such as Forward (FD), Back (BK), Right turn (RT) and Left turn (LT) to follow a teacher directed path. By assigning a numerical value to each command, students can follow a path or create their own.
2. After "playing turtle", students can transfer those commands to a paper-pencil activity and finally to a program that can be displayed on a computer when "loaded in LOGO".
3. When measuring turns in a closed path, the angle measured is the exterior angle.
4. On the second worksheet in this series, the distance between two dots is considered to be worth 5 units. While this numerical assignment is not accurate for the diagonal measurement between two points, we allow the two diagonal moves to counter balance one another rather than cloud the experience with something new at this point.
5. In the LOGO environment large problems can be broken down into smaller segments and then reassembled into a solution for a larger problem. Students can create various geometric shapes by converting what they want the turtle to draw into "turtle talk". This requires that they think sequentially.

## VII. Management Suggestions
1. It is important that students assess the turtle's heading and position before and after each command. Each turn must begin at 0 when using the "hands-on protractor."
2. You may wish to relate "turtle turns" to points on a compass or hands on a clock to help establish a visual image of 90° turns or quarter turns.

## VIII. Procedure
1. Prepare transparencies of the "turtle" and protractor so that each student has a clear copy of each.
2. Assemble turtle and protractor by centering clear turtle on top of protractor. Punch a hole in the center of both the turtle and the protractor and join both parts with a small sewing snap allowing the turtle to freely rotate around the protractor.
3. Introduce the idea of simple commands by "playing turtle" where each student is the turtle and the teacher gives the commands: Forward, Back, Right turn, Left turn. In order to know how far to move, numbers are used with each command. For example: Forward 5 means move in a forward direction 5 steps or 5 units. Each command always includes a direction and a numerical value. For turns, begin with 90° turns (a quarter of a circle).
4. Use the transparent "turtle protractor" unit to practice measuring turns or angles (see worksheet Trying Turtle Turns). Always align nose of turtle with zero on the protractor and position it on solid line (arrow). Center the snap on the vertex of the angle to be measured. Rotate only the turtle to align with the dotted line (other side of the angle) and read the number of degrees "turned". A Right turn moves from the left side of the angle to the right side of the angle and a Left turn moves from the right side of the angle to the left side of the angle. Record direction of the turn and the number of degrees.

5. Use simple commands to write the procedure for a prescribed "turtle trip" (see worksheet Try a Turtle Trip). Put two commands on each line. For example: FD 5 RT 90.

6. Draw and describe your own turtle trip (see worksheet Take a Turtle Trip).

7. If computers are available, load appropriate LOGO language disk and try same procedure. Compare paper-pencil monitor to computer print out.

## IX. **What the Students Will Do**

1. Play "turtle" to become familiar with simple LOGO commands.

2. Construct a transparent turtle and protractor to measure angles or turtle turns.

3. Write a procedure that describes a given closed path.

4. Write a procedure that draws a closed path of one's own design.

5. Apply created procedure to computer.

## X. **Discussion**

1. How can the Total Turtle Trip Theorem be explained?

## XI. **Extensions**

1. Choose any regular polygon. Write a procedure that draws that shape.

2. Use a combination of procedures to draw a picture that is composed of many shapes.

3. Write a procedure that draws a shape and then repeats or tessellates that shape on the monitor or page.

78

**PIECES AND PATTERNS**

# TURTLE TRIPS

*patterns and protractors*

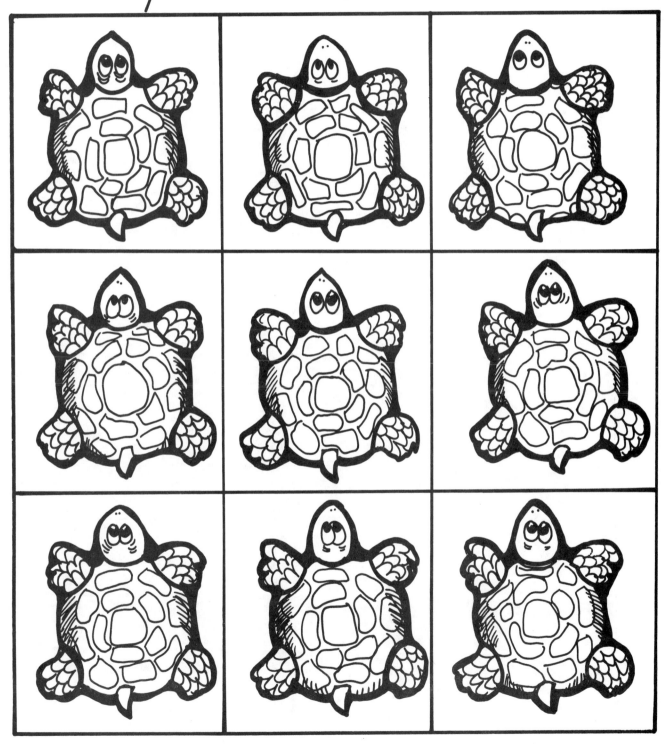

79

# TURTLE TRIPS

## patterns and protractors...

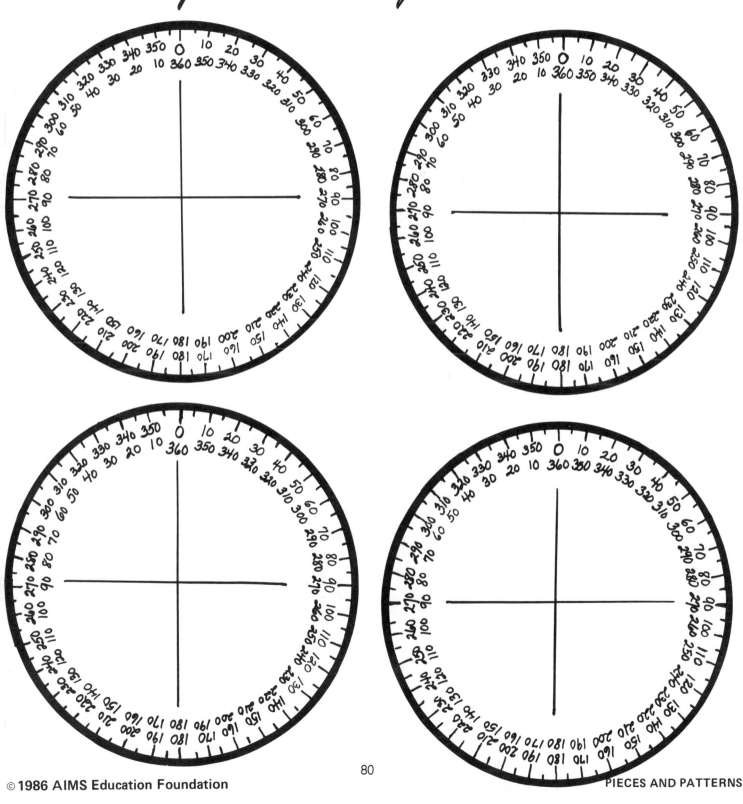

PIECES AND PATTERNS

# Trying Turtle Turns

Ⓢ Represents turtle in starting position

- - - → Represents new direction

Procedure:
1. For each turtle turn, give 2 commands and circle the most efficient one!
2. Use your transparent turtle to measure the number of degrees in each turn.
3. Remember to indicate direction and degrees .......

Example  ☐1.  (RT 90°)  or  LT 270°

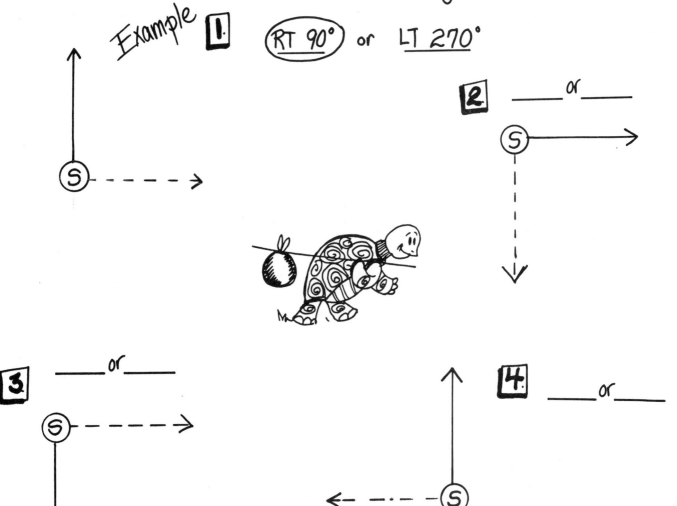

**PIECES AND PATTERNS**

# Trying Turtle Turns

5. _____ or _____

6. _____ or _____

7. _____ or _____

8. _____ or _____

9. _____ or _____

10. _____ or _____

Turtle Trivia: 1. Add the degrees of both commands. The sum is always _____°.

2. When a turtle makes one complete trip (360°) we call this the "total turtle trip theorem."

82

PIECES AND PATTERNS

# Try a Turtle Trip

Name _____

Use simple commands :  FD  FORWARD   RT  RIGHT TURN
                       BK  BACK       LT  LEFT TURN

1. Each space between 2 dots is 5 units.
2. Turtle should be in "start" or "home" position facing "north" (top of page or screen)
3. Describe turns efficiently (less than 180°)
4. Use your transparent Turtle and write the procedure for the "total trip."

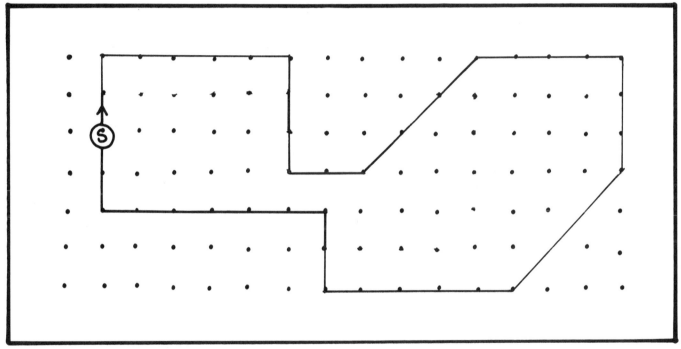

<u>FD 10 RT 90</u> _____  _____  _____  _____

_____  _____  _____  _____

_____  _____  _____  _____

_____  _____  _____  _____

Total Turtle Trip Theorem: (Turtle says  RT <sup>(sum of)</sup> — LT <sup>(sum of)</sup> = 360°)
  Add all the right turns (RT) _____
  Subtract all the left turns (LT) _____
  Turtle says you should  get : _____ (yes or no)
Why? _____

83

**PIECES AND PATTERNS**

# Take a Turtle Trip

Draw and describe a total Turtle Trip.
Use these simple commands:

| | |
|---|---|
| FORWARD | FD |
| BACK | BK |
| RIGHT | RT |
| LEFT | LT |

1. Mark the place where you begin Ⓢ
2. Connect the dots with straight lines.
3. Let the space between dots equal 5 units.
4. Do not cross your own path.
5. Be sure to end at "Home" or "Start".

Draw Your Turtle Trip Here:

Describe your trip here: (Use "Turtle Talk")

PIECES AND PATTERNS

# Rally Round the Room

### I. Topic Area
Kinetic energy, inclined planes and friction.

### II. Introductory Statement
Students will use Hot Wheels or Match Box type cars to explore concepts of friction, kinetic energy and distance traveled off an inclined plane.

### III. Math Skills                   Science Processes
a. Measuring length and        a. Observing
   weight                               b. Recording data
b. Problem solving                 c. Comparing variables
c. Logic                                 d. Interpreting data
d. Whole number                   e. Generalizing
   computation
e. Graphing
f. Range, median, mean

### IV. Materials
Cars—Hot Wheels © Mattel trademark or Match
   Box type
Inclined plane
Meter tape
Balance scale with gram weights

### V. Key Question
Which car travels the farthest? Why?

### VI. Educative Input
1. Setting up a track or inclined plane: Height of the ramp is half the length of the hypotenuse (half an equilateral triangle).

2. There is a temptation to attempt to measure speed applying the formulate $S = d/t$. Because of factors of acceleration and deceleration, only average speeds could be calculated. Therefore, this activity involves only distance traveled.
3. Several options are available for constructing the inclined plane:
   a. Simply use textbooks stacked to the desired height (half the length of the hypotenuse) and use a piece of plywood for track.
   b. Have shop teacher build a similar track from scrap lumber.

### VII. Management Suggestions
1. Students might enjoy working in teams of 2 or 3 as a driver and pit crew. It would be helpful to discuss and agree upon "job descriptions" to encourage responsible behavior and accurate measurements.
2. Agree upon fair ways to measure distance. You may wish to suggest measuring from point X to front wheels of car at rest.

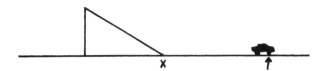

### VIII. Procedure
1. Set up track as described under Educative Input. Mark inclined plane at four evenly spaced intervals and label: Point A, B, C, and D. These will serve as release points for each of the cars entered in the Rally.
2. Have students "register" for the rally by identifying their cars by number, name of driver and crew members.
3. Students will record specifications of their cars: type, color, length and weight.
4. Students will release cars from each marked point on the inclined plane three times and record distance traveled. Then figure average distance.
5. Construct a bar graph to show distances traveled from each release point.
6. Show range, median, and mean distance from each release point in Technical Data Table.
7. Enter average distances in class "Car and Driver Test Results."
8. Apply by entering "Rally Round the Room". Events are described on student worksheet.

**PIECES AND PATTERNS**

## IX. What the Students Will Do

1. Register for Rally Round the Room by identifying and recording "specs" of their entry cars.
2. Release cars from each marked point on the inclined plane three times and record distance traveled. Find average distance.
3. Construct bar graph to show distances traveled.
4. Enter average distances in class Test Results.
5. Enter "Rally"...Events are described on Student Worksheet.

## XI. Discussion

1. Do all cars travel the same distance?
2. What factors seem to influence how far a car will travel? (weight of car, release point on inclined plane, wheels.)
3. How can I modify my car to change the distance traveled? (Try adding more weight like clay or a magnet).
4. What effect does the height of the inclined plane have on the distance traveled by a car?
5. At what release point on the inclined plane will your car travel the farthest?

## XI. Extensions

1. Change the slope of the inclined plane and compare results.
2. Measure time to distance in seconds of each car, i.e. 0-50 cm in _____ seconds.
3. Instead of cars, use marbles or balls and compare results.

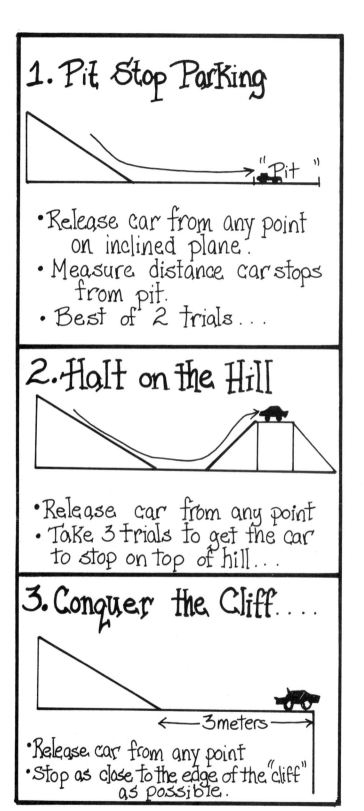

1. Pit Stop Parking
- Release car from any point on inclined plane.
- Measure distance car stops from pit.
- Best of 2 trials...

2. Halt on the Hill
- Release car from any point
- Take 3 trials to get the car to stop on top of hill...

3. Conquer the Cliff....
←— 3 meters —→
- Release car from any point
- Stop as close to the edge of the "cliff" as possible.

PIECES AND PATTERNS

# Rally Round the Room

### Rally Readiness:

Driver_____

Pit Crew_____

- Register for the Rally:
    1. Enter car number and name of driver.
    2. Measure and record specifications of vehicle.
        a. type
        b. color
        c. weight (in grams)
        d. length (in centimeters)

| Car Number | Driver Name | Specifications (Specs) | | | | Distance Traveled | | | | |
|---|---|---|---|---|---|---|---|---|---|---|
| | | Type | Color | Weight | Length | A | B | C | D | |
| | | | | g | cm | cm | cm | cm | cm | Trial 1 |
| | | | | | | cm | cm | cm | cm | Trial 2 |
| | | | | | | cm | cm | cm | cm | Trial 3 |
| | | | | | | cm | cm | cm | cm | Average |

- On your mark! Get set! Go!
    1. Release car from starting point A on inclined plane.
    2. Measure and record distance from point X to front wheel position of car at rest.
    3. Repeat two more times from point A to determine an average distance traveled.
    4. Repeat steps 1-3 from points B, C, and D on inclined plane.

# Performance Graph

- Make a bar graph that shows the distances traveled by your car from each release point.
- Indicate scale to show distance traveled.
  - one square = _____ cm. Calibrate horizonal axis.
- Shade in distance traveled for each trial.

Trial

| | | |
|---|---|---|
| A | 1 2 3 | |
| B | 1 2 3 | |
| C | 1 2 3 | |
| D | 1 2 3 | |

Distance Traveled in centimeters

## Technical Data Table

- Enter:

  1. Range of distances traveled:

  2. Median distance traveled:

  3. Mean distance traveled:

| A | B | C | D |
|---|---|---|---|
| | | | |
| | | | |
| | | | |

88

PIECES AND PATTERNS

# Car and Driver Test Results

| Car # | Driver/Crew | "Specs" | | | | Distance Average | | | |
|---|---|---|---|---|---|---|---|---|---|
| | | Type | Color | Weight | Length | A | B | C | D |
| 1. | 1. _____ 2. _____ | | | g | cm | | | | |
| 2. | 1. _____ 2. _____ | | | g | cm | | | | |
| 3. | 1. _____ 2. _____ | | | g | cm | | | | |
| 4. | 1. _____ 2. _____ | | | g | cm | | | | |
| 5. | 1. _____ 2. _____ | | | g | cm | | | | |
| 6. | 1. _____ 2. _____ | | | g | cm | | | | |
| 7. | 1. _____ 2. _____ | | | g | cm | | | | |
| 8. | 1. _____ 2. _____ | | | g | cm | | | | |
| 9. | 1. _____ 2. _____ | | | g | cm | | | | |
| 10. | 1. _____ 2. _____ | | | g | cm | | | | |
| 11. | 1. _____ 2. _____ | | | g | cm | | | | |
| 12. | 1. _____ 2. _____ | | | g | cm | | | | |
| 13. | 1. _____ 2. _____ | | | g | cm | | | | |
| 14. | 1. _____ 2. _____ | | | g | cm | | | | |

1. Which 3 cars traveled the farthest? _____ _____ _____

2. What do they have in common? _____

_____

3. How can I modify my car to go further? _____

_____

# Rally Round the Room

Driver: _____

Car: _____

| Description of Event | Scoring Procedure | Score |
|---|---|---|

## Description of Event

### 1. Pit Stop Parking

"Pit"

- Release car from any point on inclined plane.
- Measure distance car stops from pit.
- Best of 2 trials...

### 2. Halt on the Hill

- Release car from any point
- Take 3 trials to get the car to stop on top of hill...

### 3. Conquer the Cliff....

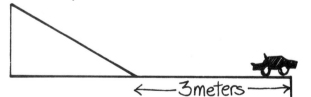

← 3 meters →

- Release car from any point
- Stop as close to the edge of the "cliff" as possible.

## Scoring Procedure

### Rally Regulations

- Car is totally in "pit"   100 pts.
- Most of car is in "pit"   75 pts.
- Car is 1-2 cm from "pit"   50 pts.
- Car is 3-4 cm from "pit"   30 pts.

- If car "halts" on the hill on:

  1st trial = 150 pts.
  2nd trial = 100 pts.
  3rd trial = 50 pts.

- If car is within edge of cliff by:

  0-2 cm  = 200 pts.
  2-4 cm  = 100 pts.
  4-6 cm  = 50 pts.
- over the cliff, subtract 50 points *

Total Performance Score

## Score

### Points

pts.

pts.

pts.

pts.

90

**PIECES AND PATTERNS**

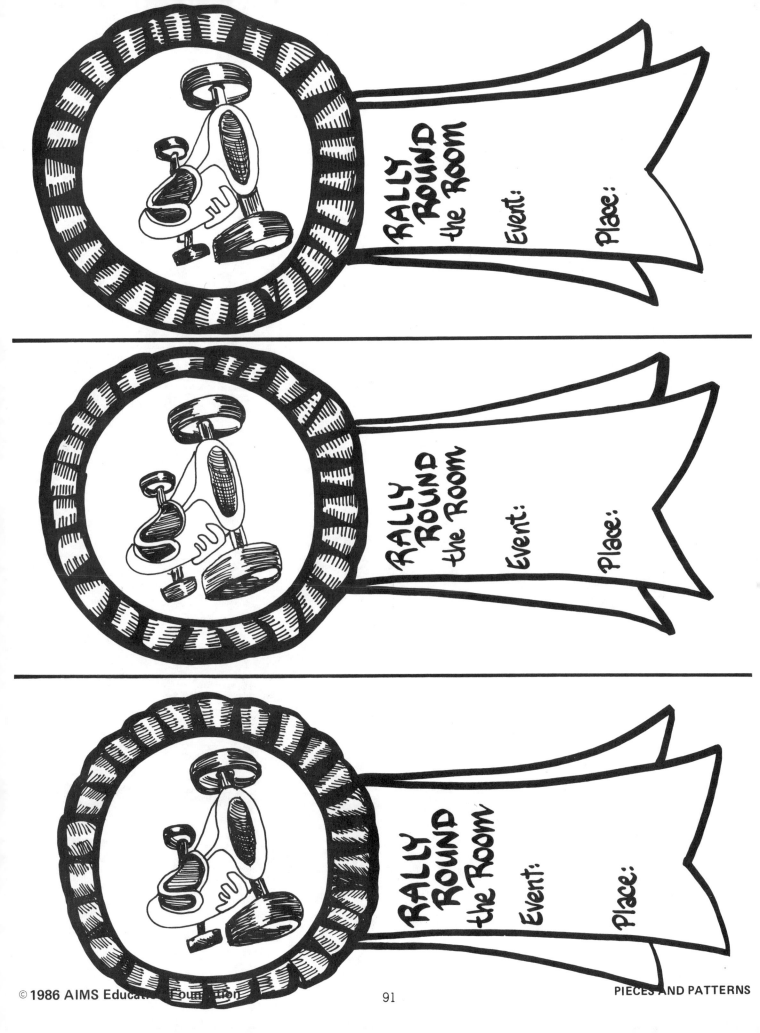

RALLY ROUND the Room

Event:

Place:

RALLY ROUND the Room

Event:

Place:

RALLY ROUND the Room

Event:

Place:

**PIECES AND PATTERNS**

# The AIMS Program

AIMS is the acronym for "Activities Integrating Mathematics and Science." Such integration enriches learning and makes it meaningful and holistic. AIMS began as a project of Fresno Pacific University to integrate the study of mathematics and science in grades K-9, but has since expanded to include language arts, social studies, and other disciplines.

AIMS is a continuing program of the non-profit AIMS Education Foundation. It had its inception in a National Science Foundation funded program whose purpose was to explore the effectiveness of integrating mathematics and science. The project directors in cooperation with 80 elemen- tary classroom teachers devoted two years to a thorough field-testing of the results and implications of integration.

The approach met with such positive results that the decision was made to launch a program to create instructional materials incorporating this concept. Despite the fact that thoughtful educators have long recommended an integrative approach, very little appropriate material was available in 1981 when the project began. A series of writing projects have ensued and today the AIMS Education Foundation is committed to continue the creation of new integrated activities on a permanent basis.

The AIMS program is funded through the sale of this developing series of books and proceeds from the Foundation's endowment. All net income from program and products flows into a trust fund administered by the AIMS Education Foundation. Use of these funds is restricted to support of research, development, and publication of new materials. Writers donate all their rights to the Foundation to support its on-going program. No royalties are paid to the writers.

The rationale for integration lies in the fact that science, mathematics, language arts, social studies, etc., are integrally interwoven in the real world from which it follows that they should be similarly treated in the classroom where we are preparing students to live in that world. Teachers who use the AIMS program give enthusiastic endorsement to the effectiveness of this approach.

Science encompasses the art of questioning, investigating, hypothesizing, discovering, and communicating. Mathematics is a language that provides clarity, objectivity, and understanding. The language arts provide us powerful tools of communication. Many of the major contemporary societal issues stem from advancements in science and must be studied in the context of the social sciences. Therefore, it is timely that all of us take seriously a more holistic mode of educating our students. This goal motivates all who are associated with the AIMS Program. We invite you to join us in this effort.

Meaningful integration of knowledge is a major recommendation coming from the nation's professional science and mathematics associations. The American Association for the Advancement of Science in *Science for All Americans* strongly recommends the integration of mathematics, science, and technology. The National Council of Teachers of Mathematics places strong emphasis on applications of mathematics such as are found in science investigations. AIMS is fully aligned with these recommendations.

Extensive field testing of AIMS investigations confirms these beneficial results.

1. Mathematics becomes more meaningful, hence more useful, when it is applied to situations that interest students.
2. The extent to which science is studied and understood is increased, with a significant economy of time, when mathematics and science are integrated.
3. There is improved quality of learning and retention, supporting the thesis that learning which is meaningful and relevant is more effective.
4. Motivation and involvement are increased dramatically as students investigate real-world situations and participate actively in the process.

We invite you to become part of this classroom teacher movement by using an integrated approach to learning and sharing any suggestions you may have. The AIMS Program welcomes you!

# AIMS Education Foundation Programs

## A Day with AIMS

Intensive one-day workshops are offered to introduce educators to the philosophy and rationale of AIMS. Participants will discuss the methodology of AIMS and the strategies by which AIMS principles may be incorporated into curriculum. Each participant will take part in a variety of hands-on AIMS investigations to gain an understanding of such aspects as the scientific/mathematical content, classroom management, and connections with other curricular areas. *A Day with AIMS* workshops may be offered anywhere in the United States. Necessary supplies and take-home materials are usually included in the enrollment fee.

## A Week with AIMS

Throughout the nation, AIMS offers many one-week workshops each year, usually in the summer. Each workshop lasts five days and includes at least 30 hours of AIMS hands-on instruction. Participants are grouped according to the grade level(s) in which they are interested. Instructors are members of the AIMS Instructional Leadership Network. Supplies for the activities and a generous supply of take-home materials are included in the enrollment fee. Sites are selected on the basis of applications submitted by educational organizations. If chosen to host a workshop, the host agency agrees to provide specified facilities and cooperate in the promotion of the workshop. The AIMS Education Foundation supplies workshop materials as well as the travel, housing, and meals for instructors.

## AIMS One-Week Perspectives Workshops

Each summer, Fresno Pacific University offers AIMS one-week workshops on its campus in Fresno, California. AIMS Program Directors and highly qualified members of the AIMS National Leadership Network serve as instructors.

## The Science Festival and the Festival of Mathematics

Each summer, Fresno Pacific University offers a Science Festival and a Festival of Mathematics. These festivals have gained national recognition as inspiring and challenging experiences, giving unique opportunities to experience hands-on mathematics and science in topical and grade-level groups. Guest faculty includes some of the nation's most highly regarded mathematics and science educators. Supplies and take-home materials are included in the enrollment fee.

## The AIMS Instructional Leadership Program

This is an AIMS staff-development program seeking to prepare facilitators for leadership roles in science/math education in their home districts or regions. Upon successful completion of the program, trained facilitators may become members of the AIMS Instructional Leadership Network, qualified to conduct AIMS workshops, teach AIMS in-service courses for college credit, and serve as AIMS consultants. Intensive training is provided in mathematics, science, process and thinking skills, workshop management, and other relevant topics.

## College Credit and Grants

Those who participate in workshops may often qualify for college credit. If the workshop takes place on the campus of Fresno Pacific University, that institution may grant appropriate credit. If the workshop takes place off-campus, arrangements can sometimes be made for credit to be granted by another institution. In addition, the applicant's home school district is often willing to grant in-service or professional-development credit. Many educators who participate in AIMS workshops are recipients of various types of educational grants, either local or national. Nationally known foundations and funding agencies have long recognized the value of AIMS mathematics and science workshops to educators. The AIMS Education Foundation encourages educators interested in attending or hosting workshops to explore the possibilities suggested above. Although the Foundation strongly supports such interest, it reminds applicants that they have the primary responsibility for fulfilling *current* requirements.

**For current information regarding the programs described above, please complete the following:**

---

### *Information Request*

Please send current information on the items checked:

\_\_\_ *Basic Information Packet* on AIMS materials     \_\_\_ *AIMS One-Week Perspectives* workshops
\_\_\_ *Festival of Mathematics*     \_\_\_ *A Week with AIMS* workshops
\_\_\_ *Science Festival*     \_\_\_ Hosting information for *A Day with AIMS* workshops
\_\_\_ *AIMS Instructional Leadership Program*     \_\_\_ Hosting information for *A Week with AIMS* workshops

Name _____ Phone _____

Address _____
       Street                City                State    Zip

---

# AIMS Program Publications

## GRADES K-4 SERIES

Bats Incredible!
Brinca de Alegria Hacia la Primavera con las Matemáticas y Ciencias
Cáete de Gusto Hacia el Otoño con la Matemáticas y Ciencias
Cycles of Knowing and Growing
Fall Into Math and Science
Field Detectives
Glide Into Winter With Math and Science
Hardhatting in a Geo-World (Revised Edition, 1996)
Jaw Breakers and Heart Thumpers (Revised Edition, 1995)
Los Cincos Sentidos
Overhead and Underfoot (Revised Edition, 1994)
Patine al Invierno con Matemáticas y Ciencias
Popping With Power (Revised Edition, 1996)
Primariamente Física (Revised Edition, 1994)
Primarily Earth
Primariamente Plantas
Primarily Physics (Revised Edition, 1994)
Primarily Plants
Sense-able Science
Spring Into Math and Science
Under Construction

## GRADES K-6 SERIES

Budding Botanist
Critters
El Botanista Principiante
Exploring Environments
Mostly Magnets
Ositos Nada Más
Primarily Bears
Principalmente Imanes
Water Precious Water

## GRADES 5-9 SERIES

Actions with Fractions
Brick Layers
Brick Layers II
Conexiones Eléctricas
Down to Earth
Electrical Connections
Finding Your Bearings (Revised Edition, 1996)
Floaters and Sinkers (Revised Edition, 1995)
From Head to Toe
Fun With Foods
Gravity Rules!
Historical Connections in Mathematics, Volume I
Historical Connections in Mathematics, Volume II
Historical Connections in Mathematics, Volume III
Just for the Fun of It!
Machine Shop
Magnificent Microworld Adventures
Math + Science, A Solution
Off the Wall Science: A Poster Series Revisited
Our Wonderful World
Out of This World (Revised Edition, 1994)
Pieces and Patterns, A Patchwork in Math and Science
Piezas y Diseños, un Mosaic de Matemáticas y Ciencias
Proportional Reasoning
Soap Films and Bubbles
Spatial Visualization
The Sky's the Limit (Revised Edition, 1994)
The Amazing Circle, Volume 1
Through the Eyes of the Explorers:
    Minds-on Math & Mapping
What's Next, Volume 1
What's Next, Volume 2
What's Next, Volume 3

For further information write to:
AIMS Education Foundation • P.O. Box 8120 • Fresno, California 93747-8120
www.AIMSedu.org/ • Fax 559•255•6396

# We invite you to subscribe to *AIMS*!

Each issue of *AIMS* contains a variety of material useful to educators at all grade levels. Feature articles of lasting value deal with topics such as mathematical or science concepts, curriculum, assessment, the teaching of process skills, and historical background. Several of the latest AIMS math/science investigations are always included, along with their reproducible activity sheets. As needs direct and space allows, various issues contain news of current developments, such as workshop schedules, activities of the AIMS Instructional Leadership Network, and announcements of upcoming publications.

*AIMS* is published monthly, August through May. Subscriptions are on an annual basis only. A subscription entered at any time will begin with the next issue, but will also include the previous issues of that volume. Readers have preferred this arrangement because articles and activities within an annual volume are often interrelated.

Please note that an *AIMS* subscription automatically includes duplication rights for one school site for all issues included in the subscription. Many schools build cost-effective library resources with their subscriptions.

---

## YES! I am interested in subscribing to *AIMS*.

Name _____  Home Phone _____

Address _____  City, State, Zip _____

Please send the following volumes (subject to availability):

| | | | | | | |
|---|---|---|---|---|---|---|
| _____ | Volume V | (1990-91) | $30.00 | _____ Volume X | (1995-96) | $30.00 |
| _____ | Volume VI | (1991-92) | $30.00 | _____ Volume XI | (1996-97) | $30.00 |
| _____ | Volume VII | (1992-93) | $30.00 | _____ Volume XII | (1997-98) | $30.00 |
| _____ | Volume VIII | (1993-94) | $30.00 | _____ Volume XIII | (1998-99) | $30.00 |
| _____ | Volume IX | (1994-95) | $30.00 | _____ Volume XIV | (1999-00) | $30.00 |

_____ **Limited offer: Volumes XIV & XV (1999-2001) $55.00**
(Note: Prices may change without notice)

**Check your method of payment:**

❏ Check enclosed in the amount of $ _____

❏ Purchase order attached (Please include the P.O.#, the authorizing signature, and position of the authorizing person.)

❏ Credit Card    ❏ Visa    ❏ MasterCard    Amount $ _____

Card # _____   Expiration Date _____

Signature _____   Today's Date _____

Make checks payable to **AIMS Education Foundation.**
Mail to *AIMS* Magazine, P.O. Box 8120, Fresno, CA 93747-8120.
Phone (559) 255-4094 or (888) 733-2467  FAX (559) 255-6396
**AIMS Homepage: http://www.AIMSedu.org/**

# AIMS Duplication Rights Program

AIMS has received many requests from school districts for the purchase of unlimited duplication rights to AIMS materials. In response, the AIMS Education Foundation has formulated the program outlined below. There is a built-in flexibility which, we trust, will provide for those who use AIMS materials extensively to purchase such rights for either individual activities or entire books.

It is the goal of the AIMS Education Foundation to make its materials and programs available at reasonable cost. All income from the sale of publications and duplication rights is used to support AIMS programs; hence, strict adherence to regulations governing duplication is essential. Duplication of AIMS materials beyond limits set by copyright laws and those specified below is strictly forbidden.

## Limited Duplication Rights

Any purchaser of an AIMS book may make up to *200 copies* of any activity in that book for use at *one school site*. Beyond that, rights must be purchased according to the appropriate category.

## Unlimited Duplication Rights for Single Activities

An individual or school may purchase the right to make an unlimited number of copies of a single activity. The royalty is $5.00 per activity per school site.

Examples:  3 activities x 1 site  x $5.00 =  $15.00
9 activities x 3 sites x $5.00 = $135.00

## Unlimited Duplication Rights for Entire Books

A school or district may purchase the right to make an unlimited number of copies of a single, *specified* book. The royalty is $20.00 per book per school site. This is in addition to the cost of the book.

Examples:  5 books x 1 site    x $20.00  =  $100.00
12 books  x 10 sites  x $20.00  =  $2400.00

## Magazine/Newsletter Duplication Rights

Those who purchase *AIMS* (magazine)/*Newsletter* are hereby granted permission to make up to 200 copies of any portion of it, provided these copies will be used for educational purposes.

## Workshop Instructors' Duplication Rights

Workshop instructors may distribute to registered workshop participants a maximum of 100 copies of any article and/or 100 copies of no more than eight activities, provided these six conditions are met:

1. Since all AIMS activities are based upon the *AIMS Model of Mathematics* and the *AIMS Model of Learning*, leaders must include in their presentations an explanation of these two models.
2. Workshop instructors must relate the AIMS activities presented to these basic explanations of the AIMS philosophy of education.
3. The copyright notice must appear on all materials distributed.
4. Instructors must provide information enabling participants to order books and magazines from the Foundation.
5. Instructors must inform participants of their limited duplication rights as outlined below.
6. Only student pages may be duplicated.

Written permission must be obtained for duplication beyond the limits listed above. Additional royalty payments may be required.

## Workshop Participants' Rights

Those enrolled in workshops in which AIMS student activity sheets are distributed may duplicate a maximum of 35 copies or enough to use the lessons one time with one class, whichever is less. Beyond that, rights must be purchased according to the appropriate category.

---

## Application for Duplication Rights

The purchasing agency or individual must clearly specify the following:
1. Name, address, and telephone number
2. Titles of the books for Unlimited Duplication Rights contracts
3. Titles of activities for Unlimited Duplication Rights contracts
4. Names and addresses of school sites for which duplication rights are being purchased.

*NOTE: Books to be duplicated must be purchased separately and are not included in the contract for Unlimited Duplication Rights.*

The requested duplication rights are automatically authorized when proper payment is received, although a *Certificate of Duplication Rights* will be issued when the application is processed.

Address all correspondence to:  **Contract Division**
**AIMS Education Foundation**
**P.O. Box 8120**
**Fresno, CA  93747-8120**

www.AIMSedu.org/
Fax 559•255•6396